D1166167

This book is courageous. It is written with great sensitivity to, and respect for, those facing aging, sickness, and death themselves; the caregivers attempting to attend to their needs; and especially the complexities of the human dynamics entailed when those realities involve family members. The author draws on her own rich experience as a coach, as a hospice worker, and most important, as someone who has lived through and learned from her own involvement with family members facing aging, illness, and death. Using these experiences, Arnup opens up new vistas for her readers, providing them with different ways of thinking about the issues that face them so that they can act authentically and realistically in the unique situations that are facing them.

—Dr. Aviva Freedman, Professor Emeritus,
   Linguistics and Language Studies,
   Carleton University

Caring for our mothers, fathers and in-laws has become a predictable part of adult life. While parent care can be a rich experience, it is difficult under the best of circumstances. Dr. Arnup deftly melds stories from her personal and professional experience to provide practical guidance and sound counsel. *I don't have time for this!* is an invaluable resource for all of us with aging parents.

—Ira Byock, MD, Director of the Providence
   Institute for Human Caring, Professor at
   Dartmouth's Geisel School of Medicine,
   author of *Dying Well* and *The Best Care Possible*

Dr. Arnup writes eloquently and sincerely about a deeply personal journey that resonated with my own experiences as a palliative care physician. Her reflections are both practical and spiritual, providing validation for difficult feelings and a roadmap for how to deal with them. Children of aging parents will find this an invaluable guide to navigating the complex and difficult task of caring for oneself while caring for dying parents.

—Andrew Mai, MD, CCFP,
    Medical Director, Ottawa Hospice Services

Katherine Arnup's book provides an important missing link for those seeking information and support on caring for elderly parents. Far more than a checklist of financial and healthcare issues to cover, it provides the compassionate companionship families need to make this journey together with love, courage, and humanity.

—Susan Piver, *New York Times* best-selling author of
    six books including *The Wisdom of a Broken Heart*
    and *The Hard Questions for Adult Children and
    Their Aging Parents*

"I don't have time for this!"

A Compassionate Guide to Caring for Your Parents and Yourself

Katherine Arnup, PhD

Life Changes Press 2015
Ottawa, Canada

Library and Archives Canada Cataloguing in Publication
Arnup, Katherine, 1949-, author
    "I don't have time for this!" : a compassionate guide to caring for your parents and yourself / by Katherine Arnup, PhD.

Includes bibliographical references.
Issued in print and electronic formats.
ISBN 978-0-9940078-0-3 (pbk.).--ISBN 978-0-9940078-1-0 (html).--
ISBN 978-0-9940078-2-7 (kindle)

    1. Aging parents--Care. 2. Parent and adult child. 3. Adult children of aging parents--Family relationships. I. Title.

HQ1063.6.A76 2015   306.874   C2015-900383-0
                                             C2015-900384-9

Contents

Preface

"You need to always remember how important this book is," the man seated beside me at the bar instructed me. "Kids today, they're selfish. They've got a million reasons why they can't help their parents out. But it's not right. You need to tell them."

Conversations like this took place all over the United States and Canada as I travelled with my manuscript, writing in coffee shops during the day and bars at night. But still, this man stood out. He was a big man, tall with the wide girth of a well-lived life. As he told me about his father, an Irish immigrant who joined the Navy to fight in the First World War, tears filled his eyes. When the war ended, his father started his own hugely successful business, despite having had only a sixth-grade education. "Excuse me," he said, dabbing his eyes with a yellow handkerchief from his pocket. "I loved him very much."

His father, it turned out, had died in 1972, more than 40 years before our chance encounter.

He continued: "After my mother died in 1962, my father told us, 'I don't want you taking care of me. The Vets will take care of me. I can go to the soldiers' home if I need to.' In the end, Dad moved in with my sister. She'd had cancer and she had no ovaries as a result, so she didn't have any kids to worry about. My sister made him feel wanted. So he did move in with her."

"Kids today," he continued, "they just see their parents as an obligation. Remember every day how important this book is."

Not everyone cries when they hear about my book, but almost everyone has a story.

If you're reading this book, I'm betting you do too.

1

"I don't have time for this!"

If you've picked up this book, chances are you have at least one elderly parent. They may already be experiencing serious health issues.

You feel overwhelmed.

You feel guilty almost all the time.

You feel as though you are always letting someone down—your partner, children, parents, co-workers, employer, friends. (You don't even include yourself on that list because you have long since given up on caring for yourself.)

You have no time.

You barely have enough time to sleep. You don't have time for the gym or a proper breakfast or an evening out with friends. When you're awake, you fixate on your to-do lists, which never seem to get done.

You're glued to your cell phone day and night, just in case of emergency—and it feels as if an emergency might happen at any time. Your mother falling in her living room and hitting her head on the coffee table. Your father wandering away from home in the middle of the night. Given the number of trips to the Emergency

Room you've made this year, it's likely that an emergency is just around the corner.

Even though you have friends in a similar position, still you feel alone. You're too ashamed to admit that you're not coping. You've always been so organized, so capable. Your nickname is "planner girl." You joke that the term multitasking was invented for you. But now you've lost your ability to focus. You need help and you have no idea where to turn.

It seemed to happen almost imperceptibly. Your father calls you by mistake, intending to dial your sister. "Dammit," he says, before hanging up without a goodbye. It's not that different: he's never had the best telephone manners. Still, when you come to think about it, you realize that this isn't the first time this sort of thing has happened. You remember the time he locked himself out of his apartment. The time the superintendent had to ask you to check up on him. The time he ended up in ER when he fell and couldn't get up. The time he was so short of breath on the walk to the restaurant that he had to sit down on the bench.

Once you see the events listed together, it seems more of a pattern than a single isolated incident. He is 90, after all. And though he managed to give a 45-minute speech without notes at his birthday celebration, still you worry when he takes the subway instead of a cab. When he walks across the mall parking lot you wince as the cars slam on their brakes to avoid hitting him. Perhaps it is time for you to take more than a passing notice.

But when? Between your job and your children, the house, the bills, and the minor illnesses you can't seem to shake off, what time have you got? You barely sleep, waking up every night at 3 a.m., with your mind racing with all the things you have to do. Most nights you get up and attend to emails: at least you can get something done without distractions. You get out of bed for a run at six, before waking your daughters, grabbing some breakfast, making the lunches and heading out to school and work. You feel lost, frightened, overwhelmed—and very much alone.

If this sounds a little like your life, this book is for you.

This book is a guide to navigating the challenging waters of being the adult children of elderly parents.

Drawing upon case studies, interviews, a compendium of research, and my own experiences when caring for my parents, this book will help you to:

- understand where this crisis in caring for our elders comes from
- step up to the plate to care for your parents
- put yourself in your parents' shoes (even though you vow that you'll never be like them!)
- feel compassionate towards your parents (even though their incessant phone calls are driving you nuts!)
- work with your siblings, children, friends and relatives to engage their support
- hold productive meetings with your family—meetings that don't end up in either tears or shouting matches
- begin to let go of guilt
- help your parents to live safe, comfortable, fulfilling lives to the end
- be kind to yourself, because this is probably the hardest thing you've ever done

Reading this book will not make your parents' aging and deaths easy or simple: that is impossible. However, I hope that it will help you come to terms with loss and fight the urge to run away to Australia.

I can't give you more than 168 hours in a week, but I can help you to identify and make time for the things that really matter to you. In fact, in being present to your parents, you will find that time slows down and that the spinning, out-of-control feeling will ease—perhaps even disappear!

This is the book I wish I had been given when my sister and my parents were dying. It's the book I hope my daughters will read, before I reach that stage of life.

2

Both sides now

I've looked at life from both sides now
—Joni Mitchell

Almost twenty years ago, my sister Carol died of cancer. She was a gifted Special Education teacher, director of countless school musicals, and my big sister. In January 1997, 19 years after her first encounter with melanoma, her cancer returned with an unstoppable force. As part of a team of friends and family, I cared for her during her final six months: the saddest, most terrifying and most transformative experience of my life.

Shortly before her death, Carol quipped, "You're going to be an expert at this by the time you're done with me."

"Maybe," I protested, "but I don't want to learn it from you!"

We both laughed, knowing that, of course, this was precisely what was happening.

I had a lot of learning to do because, before my sister got sick, I was more terrified of death than you can imagine.

I was the kind of person who rarely sent sympathy cards,

disdaining their saccharine sentiments, yet lacking the appropriate words myself. Upon hearing that someone's father had died, I would give them a wide berth, telling myself that I didn't know what to say. I was secretly afraid that just talking about death might draw me closer to my own mortality. I blamed my shyness, my temperament, and my WASP upbringing, but, of course, it was really fear.

Caring for my sister as she was dying transformed me. From a person who would run screaming from the room at the thought of loss, I found myself comforting people who had lost someone they loved. Slowly, almost without my noticing it, I began to accept—not only know—that death was something we all have in common. Four years after her death, I took the volunteer training course at a local residential hospice program. From the moment I walked into the hospice, I knew that it was where I belonged. It was an almost eerie feeling. Yet week after week, as I returned for my shift, I found myself increasingly at home, talking to family members, caring for dying people, helping to teach others what my sister had taught me.

Each week, I see other people doing things they never thought they could do. Providing physical care and comfort. Sitting at the bedside of an elderly parent. Being a witness to the suffering of someone they love. Letting go of the minutiae that tend to dominate our lives—billable hours, email, Twitter, endless to-do lists. I see people sitting in silence, holding the hand of someone they love, offering a drink of water, singing a song. These are the things my sister taught me. And now, these are the things I teach others. I tell them it is an honour to care for someone you love. Challenging as it may be, it is also something they will never regret.

I was 47 when my sister died (she was 51). Though often scared that I might not be able to endure the situation, my love for her enabled me to face my own fear of cancer, illness—even death itself. In facing those fears which had both dominated and limited my life, I was able to bring comfort to hospice patients and their families, to friends and relatives facing their parents' aging. And I was empowered to face my own parents' final years when that time came.

In fact, my sister's illness was not my first experience with a life-threatening illness. Seven years before, my mother had suffered a devastating brain aneurysm which had left her profoundly disabled, unable to walk, unable to care for herself, and unable to communicate easily. Though I visited her out of a sense of obligation, I found her condition extremely upsetting—so much so that I avoided being with her as much as possible. After Carol died, however, I found myself much more comfortable with our mother. It turned out that I was the one with whom she could most easily confide about our joint loss. On visits with Mom, we would cry as we talked about how much we missed Carol. Years later, after my father's death, once again my mother and I could share in our grief and sorrow. Strangely enough, I wasn't afraid anymore.

In this book, you will also encounter my father: a man who had made it to 92 almost unscathed. We used to joke that Dad had never met an obstacle he couldn't overcome. That was, until he developed Myelodysplastic Syndrome, a terminal blood disorder that renders the bones incapable of producing red blood cells. Over the next two years, my father suffered a series of heart attacks and was forced to endure almost weekly blood transfusions to mitigate the effects of his disease. In his final five months, he required oxygen, a walker, and round-the-clock caregivers. Throughout his illness, until his death at 94, I was a frequent visitor, sitting and talking with him, watching television with him, and—inevitably, day by day—witnessing his painfully slow decline.

Just ten days after his death, my mother was diagnosed with terminal lung cancer, and I was once again called upon to accompany a family member on their final journey. Again, my sister's lessons served me well. I was able to comfort my mother about the loss of her husband, to bring her Timbits and to watch the Blue Jays throw away another game. And on the night before she died, I climbed into her hospital bed, to comfort her and sing to her while the morphine slowly eased her pain.

Through my work as a hospice volunteer and in my relationships with friends and family members, I've been able to carry the message that aging, illness, and dying need not be scary. Instead they are a natural part of life, just as much as birth is, or coming of age. And when we face our fears, when we stop running away long enough to pay attention and be fully present with the people we care for, our own lives can also be transformed. The grip that fear had on us is loosened. Our relationships deepen, and our time with the people we love becomes much more precious.

Helping people to come to terms with life's transitions, including illness, aging, and death, has gradually become my life's work. Through my teaching, writing, coaching, and hospice volunteering, I bring the message that facing our fears enables us to place the pressures of our lives into true perspective. I also believe that death reminds us of the importance of living in every moment.

The time has come to bring this message to the world. I wrote this book because I have seen how I have been able to help people to come to terms with their parents' aging and increasing need for support and care. I have helped people to stop running away from these responsibilities and relationships, and to face head-on the fears that their parents' neediness raises for them. Through confronting these fears, you too can face those adversities that life sends your way, and see life's inevitable challenges and transitions as opportunities to enrich your life.

As I write this book, I find myself in a peculiar position. On the one hand, I am no longer an adult child caring for aging parents (since my parents died nearly a decade ago, and with their passing, those duties ended). On the other, at 65, I am not yet an aging parent in need of care from my own adult children.

Still, I can viscerally recall what it felt like, to be caring for and worrying constantly about my elderly parents. And I can see, just beyond the horizon, to the time when my daughters will themselves be coming to terms with how to care for their fiercely independent, rather quirky mother.

Most books on caregiving are written from the point of view of an adult child caring for an aging parent. Indeed, I began this book from that perspective. The realization that I'm on both sides now took me by surprise and only after I recovered from the shock did I realize the huge advantage this dual perspective affords. I understand completely when one of my clients complains about the endless trips she makes in order to care for her elderly and increasingly infirm mother. I hear her fatigue, frustration, and impatience. I also know that one day there will be no more trips to make. (She knows this too, but only vaguely at this point.) And I also know that one day she will be hoping that her daughter or son will bring the grandchildren to visit more frequently, and that they'll be close by when she has surgery, tests, or treatment. How she will passionately hope that she can count on them when she needs them, without being a burden.

I hope that, by reading this book, you can gain something of this perspective as well. I hope that it will help you to slow down and to be a little more patient with your elderly parents—and to help you to be kinder to yourself. I hope that it will enable you to be more present, so that you don't miss the small joys and special moments that you will encounter along the road.

3

How did we end up here?

Whenever I have found myself in a circumstance in life, the origins of which I can't fully explain, I have turned to historical research for answers. When I had my first child in 1982, six weeks before I began my PhD program—it seemed like a good idea at the time!—I found myself struggling with mountains of conflicting advice about how best to feed and care for a newborn baby. 'What did women do before all these experts existed?' I wondered.

The question led me to research the history of infant and child-rearing advice for mothers in the United States, Canada, and Britain throughout the 19th and 20th centuries: the subject of my doctoral dissertation and eventually my first book, *Education for Motherhood*.

When my older daughter reached thirteen, I began to wonder how people had dealt with their teenagers in the age before the internet, Mommy Blogs, and Dr. Phil. Unfortunately (or perhaps fortunately, for them!) both my girls were well beyond their teenage years before I had time to contemplate that research, and by then, it had been supplanted by other, more pressing, issues.

A decade or so ago, as an exhausted member of the sandwich

generation, I began to ask other questions. How did we end up here? Did I do something wrong? Did my parents? To find answers, I began to research the history and origins of care for the elderly, ill, and dying. My research led to a series of public talks, articles, and now, this book. My curiosity, it seems, always results in more work for me—although, with luck, also in benefits for my readers and clients.

Open any newspaper these days and you'll likely find an article on the "crisis of aging" facing our society. If you are under 40, you are probably shaking your head, wondering if there's going to be any money left in Social Security or the Canada Pension Plan by the time you retire. If you're a little older, you're probably already swept up in the crisis, as your aging parents enter their "golden years." And if you're a Baby Boomer, chances are you're wondering how this happened to you. How did you get to be a senior citizen so soon? And if you're among the 25% of people over 60 with at least one living parent, how on earth did you get to be a senior citizen with elderly parents?

If you are wondering how people faced these issues in the past, you're not alone. The fact is that the situation that we face today is unique in human history. Let's examine its origins and key dynamics.

The unprecedented population bulge known as the Baby Boom (those people born between 1946 and 1964) is now entering retirement age and "early old age." The Baby Boom represents the largest population bulge in human history and it will likely be the largest ever.

Men and women, weary of the deprivation of the Great Depression—not to mention the losses involved in two World Wars—enthusiastically embraced marriage and domesticity, producing children at a rate not seen since the late 19th century. Families with four or more children swiftly began to appear in the rapidly spreading suburbs across North America. Furthermore, as a result of improvements in sanitation and nutrition (coupled with scientific and medical discoveries) infant mortality dropped to record lows, with the result that most families could expect to see all their offspring reach adulthood.

Widespread prosperity, along with discoveries such as antibiotics (which enabled physicians to treat diseases like pneumonia as well as life-threatening infections), vaccines (combatting polio and measles, mumps, and rubella), and surgical advances (open-heart surgery, organ transplants) not only resulted in a decrease in infant mortality rates but also in dramatic increases in life expectancy. "The average Canadian born in 2009 can be expected to live 81.2 years.... The average American will live to be just over 78."

Prior to the Second World War, most elderly people were cared for by their families or, in cases of destitution, were housed in institutions modelled on British workhouses. Following the war, Canada and the United States witnessed a tremendous expansion of hospitals and medical services, and the construction of seniors' facilities (often termed old age homes).

As illness, death and dying moved from the home into hospitals, far removed from family and daily life, most people rarely saw a dying person or a dead body. As a consequence, the fear and the avoidance of confronting death grew. By the same measure, as the elderly were routinely moved into nursing homes, many people grew uncomfortable with the very presence of older people and unfamiliar with the wisdom and value of the elderly.

For most of human history, people have recognized that life and death are inextricably linked and that aging is as natural as birth, and as much a part of life. The notion of death as the natural conclusion to life is rarely a subject of conversation today, even within families, as if somehow we can avoid its inevitability by refusing to acknowledge its existence. Instead, a virtual cult of youth and vigour, epitomized by Bob Dylan's famous song title, "(May you stay) forever young," has replaced the respect and reverence once enjoyed by elders.

Other social changes have also contributed to the crisis in caregiving we are experiencing today.

In marked contrast to the 1950s, the vast majority of women in North America are now working full-time in the paid labour force throughout their child-rearing years. At the same time, however, as the traditional caregivers within the family, they are still expected to assume responsibility for aging parents, and often parents-in-law. (As a recent Princeton University study confirmed, women still do the lion's share of caregiving for both their children and the elderly.) This generation of women is often called the sandwich generation—squeezed between two generations of people in need of their care. Their stress is compounded by the move back to the family home by many children in their 20s and even 30s, following graduation from university, a divorce, or job loss: a phenomenon that is only extending women's years of provision for their children. Indeed, women may find themselves caring for young children at home, adult children returning home, their aging parents, and a spouse (or themselves) facing serious health issues of their own.

Though geographic mobility has long been a characteristic of North Americans, the ease of air travel and the employment mobility characteristic of the global economy have meant that adult children often live vast distances from their parents, during the time when the latter are most in need of care and support. As a result, the care of elderly parents often falls upon one or two adult children who may live close by, while the other children may manage to avoid these responsibilities. For those in the post-Baby Boom generation, this problem is compounded by a relatively low birth rate, meaning there are fewer adult children to share caregiving responsibilities.

With ever-expanding health care budgets and ballooning deficits threatening all levels of government by the 1990s, communities across Canada and the United States experienced the closure of hospital beds and of small community hospitals, along with mergers and greater specialization of urban hospitals. Shorter hospital stays, an increase in the number and range of outpatient procedures, and a move towards pharmaceutical treatments for mental illness and other conditions, all had a dramatic impact on families.

In all areas of health care, deinstitutionalization effectively meant that patients were sent home. The home was once again deemed to be the place to care for family members, whether they were suffering from a terminal illness, recuperating from surgery, living with mental illness or severely disabled. In the absence of adequate home care services, and without being able to rely upon the support of an extended family or community network, families (and especially women in families) began to experience the crushing demands of caregiving—for children, elderly parents, ill family members—combined with the demands of full-time employment. This pressure would only increase by the turn of the 21st century.

With the divorce rate hovering at 50% in the United States and between 35 and 40% in Canada, blended families are an increasingly common family form. What is your responsibility for your former mother-in-law, someone who may have been "Mom" for 20 or even 30 years before your divorce, and who is still your children's grandmother?

All these factors have led to the crisis in caregiving that we are confronting today.

Canada and the United States face an unprecedented population shift, characterized by a dramatic increase in the number of people over 65—and an even more dramatic increase in people over 80. In 2011, there were 5,825 centenarians in Canada, an increase of 25.7% since 2006. The 2010 US census indicated that there were 53,364 people over 100, most of them women. While this might appear to be wonderful news, unfortunately, advanced age does not come with eternal youth.

Despite our hopes that we might remain vibrant and youthful, the reality is that more people are living (and living much longer) with chronic illnesses, disabilities, and complex medical conditions for which they require increasing amounts of care, support and intervention. As a consequence, far more old—and very old—people are relying on increasingly complex and demanding care. This care is often provided by family members, including elderly spouses, siblings, adult offspring and grandchildren, most of whom who are largely unprepared for the tasks ahead.

Given the increasing longevity of our population, Baby Boomers may well reach retirement age and beyond with aging parents needing their assistance and support. And the challenge will be even greater for the children of Baby Boomers.

We can't change these demographic realities.

We *can* change how we show up in our lives and in the lives of our children and our parents.

This book will help you to do that.

In providing you with this history, I hope that you will read this book secure in the knowledge that the situation you and your parents are facing is not the result of your failure to plan. It's not your parents' fault either. No one expected that they would live this long. And social policies have neither anticipated nor kept pace with these enormous changes.

You are in good company now. Hang on because it's going to be a bumpy ride!

4

This happens in other people's families, not mine!

The beginning…

Most of the time your caregiving "journey" will begin with a medical event—a heart attack, difficulty breathing, a fall (with broken bones), pain that won't go away (eventually leading to a cancer diagnosis). But there have probably been small indications that something is awry for months or even years that you've been trying to brush off as normal signs of your parents' aging.

Warning signs that their lives and your role
are about to change
- frequent phone calls asking for advice or help
- a lengthy list of errands for you each time you visit
- falls and injuries
- problems navigating stairs
- difficulty keeping up with the housework, yard work, maintenance of their home

- difficulty with the activities of daily living: shopping, bathing, cooking, feeding, dressing
- problems driving (unexplained dents in the car; an accident)
- forgetfulness and increasing memory issues
- sudden or unexplained health issues
- loss of appetite, weight loss
- empty fridge or rotting food in the fridge or on the counter
- financial issues: forgetting to pay bills, having difficulty keeping accounts, running out of money, running up large expenses on credit cards, becoming a victim of fraud

While you might be able to ignore one or two of these signs, if there are several or they are coupled with a medical event requiring a hospital visit, you know it's time to pay more attention to your parents' health and well-being.

Watching our parents' slow decline can be an impossibly sad and difficult experience. Even if we have a troubled relationship with them—perhaps especially if this is the case—we dread seeing them becoming someone other than the capable adult figure in our lives. How can this be happening? How can my father no longer remember what he said five minutes ago? Why is my mother obsessing about the tiniest household details? Do I really have to deal with this right now?

For those who are part of the "sandwich generation," these challenges may be especially acute. Torn between our jobs, our children, and the ever-increasing needs of our parents, thoughts of escape are common.

As parents, we raise our children (with the exception of those with serious health issues or disabilities that preclude independent living) with the knowledge—or at least the hope—that they will become increasingly independent over time, until finally they are fully independent of us, with lives and families of their own.

With our parents, unless they die of a heart attack or other sudden event (a fate, whether desirable or not, relating to only 10% of the population) we begin to recognize that they will become increasingly frail and dependent as they age, until finally they die. And the pace of their aging and deterioration can seem excruciatingly slow.

Caregiving, especially of an elderly person, is unpredictable, at times frustratingly so. Just when you think you're getting the hang of it, something happens—a fall, a new symptom, a bad medical report—and you find yourself frantically trying to adjust to the "new normal." Perhaps more than at any time in your life—except birth and babyhood—change is the only constant when you are dealing with aging, terminal illness, and dying.

While some people might claim to thrive on change, few would respond the same way if they were told that the landscape, direction, speed, and duration of that change was entirely out of their hands. The reality of cancelled appointments, missed meetings and family commitments, coupled with repeated travel—on full fare because almost always last-minute—sinks in quickly once you are dealing with an elderly parent.

Providing care for your parents is a long-term project. You are not going to be able to swoop in and wrap everything up with a few phone calls. In fact, your parents may resent your making the phone calls, even if they asked for your help! They might even undo all the arrangements for care and help you've put in place as soon as you leave their house. You will find many examples of this behaviour in the chapters that follow.

In this chapter, I consider the most common issues that arise during the early days of caring for your parents, offering some tools and strategies to help you take steps to ensure your parents' safely and independence.

One of the first things you should do when you realize your parents may need your assistance is to make an assessment of their situation.

- Are they living on their own?
- What supports do they currently have in place?
- Whose counsel do they trust and value?
- Have they asked for help?

Armed with this information, you can begin to establish some priorities for your parents (and yourself). Be sure to include your parents at every stage of the deliberations. Even though you may be certain that you know what is best for them, they will almost certainly reject any plans that you try to impose.

For most people as they age, these priorities can be considered under the following topics:

- Safety
- Independence
- Dignity and respect
- Comfort and symptom control

Safety

The first priority is to keep yourself and your parents safe. It won't be easy. They may resist your efforts, they may rebel, act out, get angry. But your response to your parents remains the same:

"It is vitally important to me that you and Mom are safe."

"I need you to be safe."

And if all else fails, "Please do this for me."

Writing this book has had some unexpected outcomes in my life. I start to notice the number of throw rugs dangerously lying in wait for an unsuspecting person (including myself) to trip on. I recognize—though I haven't eliminated—my habit of putting things on the stairs that need to be taken to the second floor, leaving them lying in wait to trip me as I race downstairs. The new cupboards we had installed in our kitchen last fall are far too high for me to reach (I'm 4' 10½" on a good day!) and my longstanding habit of climbing onto the counter to reach the top shelf is perhaps past its "best before" date. The list is long: the tub doesn't have anti-skid grippers and we don't use a bath mat; there's no grab bar either. I've noticed that I've started banging into things with more regularity than usual—misestimating their exact location in relation to my body. I blame my progressive lenses—which may be part of the problem—but surely they can't be to blame for all my bruises! And I haven't even mentioned the absence of a ground floor bathroom!

Many of our homes—especially older homes—were not designed with older people in mind. I suspect that the first owner of my home (built in 1923) didn't live to see 60 years of age. I know that many children would have grown up in this home and, possibly, a few people have died. But none of them would have been thinking about the importance of "aging in place," the currently preferred term referring to the policy of enabling people to remain in their homes for as long as possible. Many of us do want to remain in our homes, and are only just beginning to realize the kinds of changes that will need to be made.

Many municipalities offer free safety audits for seniors, to assist them in determining what changes might make it easier for them to remain in their homes. (That way your parents don't have to take your word for it. They can rely on an expert!) Furthermore, some jurisdictions—including Ontario, the province where I live—offer tax credits to offset the cost of renovations that enable a person 65 and older to remain in their home. (Examples: grab bars in the tub and by the toilet, walk-in showers, ramps to the front door, ground floor bathrooms, lower counters.)

Safety can involve everything from safety in the home (and the issues I mentioned above) to driving, taking public transit, going out alone at night—or eventually even during the day—avoiding unscrupulous fraudsters who prey on the elderly, drinking alcohol, correct use of medications, and many other issues.

The biggest challenge is not cost, inability to make changes, or the lack of resources or know-how. The biggest challenge is the chasm between your perspective of the dangers (as an adult child) and your parents' perspective of their independence and the importance of having control over their lives.

Driving

For most North Americans, perhaps nothing symbolizes freedom and independence more than driving. Remember when you were finally able to get your learner's permit? Remember how it felt to finally be able to sit behind the wheel (when the car was turned on?) Remember how proud you felt when you passed your driver's test and were finally allowed to take the car out by yourself? I can still remember taking my mother's car out for a spin on the highway, the music cranked up to top volume, all four speakers blaring. I felt as if I was finally free.

The ability to drive lets you get up and go whenever you want—to load all your belongings in the car and just drive away.

To demonstrate the power of driving in our national psyche, only a few years ago I asked my university freshman students at what stage would they want someone to "pull the plug?"

One earnest young man, an avid hockey player, immediately replied, "When I can't drive anymore." For him, having the car keys taken away meant that life wasn't worth living.

However, an ever-increasing number of people in North America are rapidly approaching that moment in their lives, whether they accept it or not. According to the National Highway Traffic Safety Administration, by 2020, there will be 40 million U.S. drivers aged 65 and over. While many of them are no doubt still competent drivers, issues involving mental and physical health are increasing every year.

A fascinating survey of 1000 people aged 75 and over, conducted by Liberty Mutual, found that the majority of those over 75 who were still driving had "increasing physical complaints" including "tiring easily, slow reaction times, difficulty in seeing or hearing, and getting lost or feeling confused while driving." Furthermore, 85% said that they avoided "driving after dark, in heavy traffic, or in unfamiliar areas."

If your parents have already given up evening or winter driving, you may already have your point of entry into a conversation about driving. If not, you may be faced with resistance, as I was with my father.

An accident

How did it happen? How did this come to be his life? In tiny increments. One day you notice you can't make out the words in the newspaper—even when you close your bad eye and squint. The cataract surgery a decade ago helped for a time, but now, even with thick glasses and eye drops twice a day, you need a magnifying glass to read the paper. Still, you can drive. Your daughters urge you to stop. "It's not safe anymore, Dad," they say. "You're going to have an accident." You nod and ignore them. How could you manage at the cottage without a car? Then one day, in broad daylight, you hit a trailer parked at the side of the highway. No one is hurt, but you are too shaken to drive the ten miles back to the cottage. The police call your eldest daughter to pick you up. On the way back to the cottage, you say little. When she presses you, you promise you will give up driving when summer's over. And though you can't imagine how, you adjust. You get used to Community Care drivers taking you grocery shopping. You adjust to depending on other people's schedules and favours. Neighbours, nieces, daughters, strangers, hired help. You don't like it. Some days you hate it so much you snap at the Community

Care worker who's helping you shop when she tries to push your grocery cart. "I may be old," you bark, "but I'm not dead yet."

My sisters and I were fortunate that my father's accident was a relatively minor one. Nothing was hurt (except his pride). But what if your parent categorically refuses to give up the keys? Their doctor can provide the necessary ammunition in cases where your parent won't listen to you or your siblings. Ask the doctor to assess your parent's eyesight, motor skills, reflexes, muscle strength, and other relevant measures affecting their ability to drive. The doctor will also consider the effect that any medications your parent is taking might have on their ability to drive safely. If your parent "fails" any of these tasks, the doctor can tell your parent to stop driving. While the doctor's view may not carry any legal force, adults of our parents' age tend to hold physicians in high esteem, and are much more likely to follow their recommendation than yours.

Some states and provinces have specific requirements for older drivers. In Ontario, for example, a driver must renew his or her licence in person at the age of 80, and must submit to an eye examination as well as attendance at an educational session on the challenges facing older drivers. Furthermore, doctors and optometrists are legally required to report a driver to the Ministry of Transportation if they feel the person has a condition that may impair their ability to drive.

Though my father did stop driving, he continued to take public transit, including the subway, which necessitated his coping with two or three flights of stairs amidst a pushing, shoving crowd. Only when he turned 92 did he agree to take a cab downtown, and only after I insisted that he really could afford it!

What about walking across a major thoroughfare (albeit one

with a traffic light) to the mall (through a busy parking lot) to get some groceries and other necessities of life? My father made this trip several times a week until a terminal blood disorder "cramped his style." Sometimes I would accompany him on these missions, as we enjoyed eating dinner together at Diana Sweets, the restaurant at the far end of the mall. I would watch the cars screech their brakes as my father set forth into the parking lot looking very much like Mr. Magoo from the cartoons of my youth. My father (like Mr. Magoo, no doubt) was legally blind (though he could read the paper by using a large magnifying glass and a flashlight trained on the page). Cars would literally veer sharply to avoid my Dad, who was blissfully unaware of the dangers. I would walk behind him (he walked more quickly than I did), waving to thank the drivers for not hitting him!

I would never have thought of telling my father that he was too old to go to the mall by himself. Not only would this have offended him deeply, but he wouldn't have listened to me anyway. I did sometimes persuade him to stick to the sidewalk rather than taking a shortcut across the parking lot, but that was the extent of my success.

Independence: **not** my parent's parent

As Baby Boomers have increasingly found themselves put in the position of caring for their own elderly parents, it has become common practice to talk about "parenting your parents." "The tables are turned now," experts proclaim. "Now it's your turn to parent your parents."

As you will not doubt have noticed, I have not suggested that you become your parents' parent. I realize that sometimes it feels as if there's been a role reversal. And it often feels that it's become your "job" to take care of them. But to see yourself as your parent's parent is to ignore the enormous history between you—whether it be largely positive or deeply troubling. And that history has not changed. Furthermore, viewing them as essentially your children is to infantilize them—definitely not what they need at this time in their life. They still see themselves as your parents, however elderly and frail they may be. And they still need to be treated with dignity and respect, especially at a time when they may feel that they are losing both. It also denies the very real feelings of sadness and grief you may be feeling as the child who will eventually lose her parents.

Single vs. couple

If both of your parents are still living, it is possible that they will be able to help one another, if only to call you if there is a crisis. If one of your parents has had to give up driving, the other one may continue to be able to drive to medical appointments, the pharmacy, the grocery store etc. Once one parent has died, however, the survivor may feel quite lost, unable to function without their other half. Also, given the gender division of labour common in our parents' generation, your remaining parent may have little or no experience in fulfilling the roles of their deceased spouse.

Of course my father was once again the exception that proves the rule. When my mother had her brain aneurysm and ultimately went to live with my eldest sister, my father adjusted easily to living alone. He had always been an excellent cook, making Sunday dinners when we were young, and in charge of most of the cooking at the cottage. Thus, cooking for himself presented no challenge. In contrast, my partner's father, had he been widowed in his 80s, would likely have had to live with one of the children, as he relied heavily on his wife for the domestic and social aspects of their lives, and was not safe living on his own when she was in the hospital.

The need for safety and the desire for independence represent the two ends of the tightrope that you will find yourself walking with your parents for the rest of their lives. In the following chapter, I will discuss how you can better understand your parents' point of view as they struggle against your efforts to keep them safe.

Can't I hire someone else to do this?

When you realize that your parents need your help and begin to take on some of the responsibilities for their care, you may find yourself longing for the "good old days," when they went about their lives and you enjoyed yours, with occasional dinners and friendly family visits. You may wish you could close your eyes and make your parents' problems disappear—or, failing that, run away. Alas, none of these alternatives will work. In fact, your efforts to cling to the past (combined with dreading the future) will make it almost impossible for you to accept the present circumstances.

"I wish they could just go to sleep one night and never wake up," my client Joanne confessed.

"And then your parents would be dead," I blurted.

"That's true, I guess, but I just hate to see them suffer like this."

Her parents, both in their 80s, were beginning to exhibit some of the signs of aging outlined at the beginning of this chapter. Living in the country, almost an hour away from the city where their daughter lived, they were finding the upkeep of the house and property more than they could manage. Since they had each other to rely upon, they were able to cope, to a degree, with her mother taking over all the driving duties since the onset of her father's mild dementia. But the calls to Joanne had increased dramatically, and requests for visits (and help with chores) had escalated too.

Joanne, a busy professional, wife, and mother who travelled frequently for her work, expressed increasing frustration, and sought coaching to help her make a plan. "It wasn't supposed to be like this," she said. "This happens in other people's families, not ours."

As we talked that day, she admitted to shame for wishing her parents would die. Though she genuinely hoped for their freedom

27

from suffering, she knew that part of her desire for the end was so that their incessant demands (and her constant worry) could be over.

Despite our best intentions and noblest aspirations, if we're honest, thoughts of escape are seldom far from our minds when we are thinking about providing care for our parents. If only they would die, peacefully and painlessly, their suffering would be over! If only I lived farther away, I wouldn't feel that I had to see them so often...

Sometimes we even pretend that we're not really dealing with our parents' decline and ultimate death.

"After Charlie does his thing, we can talk about our plans," my partner said, often prone to reducing difficult life events into tasks to be checked off her to-do list.

"You mean, dies," I said, ever the reality check (and sometimes Ms. Smarty Pants).

With my own parents, I experienced three different pathways towards the end. At 71, a massive brain aneurysm left my mother completely dependent on others for her care and survival, utterly unable to feed, dress, walk, speak clearly, wash herself, or remember vital events. Though she lived for nearly seventeen years after that event, my horror at the changes the aneurysm had wrought remained almost until the end.

Not my mother

How do you describe the first time you change your mother's diaper? Or the first time you realize that your mother's diaper needs changing?

And there is so much more. She needs to be fed. Food dribbles out of her mouth. You lean down to kiss her, but her mouth is covered in food and drool and you know it will get on your clothing, your mouth, and you long to wipe it all off as soon as you've kissed her. Then you worry that this is shameful in itself, that it represents a lack of love. Love should be unconditional and here you are wishing that this woman, your mother, did not have food all over her clothes, did not drool as she sits and stares blankly at you. You try to look in her eyes, to ignore how she looks—but you can't.

Before her massive brain aneurysm, it used to bother you that your parents' bathroom was dirty. You would see a spot of toothpaste in the sink, a drop of urine on the toilet seat and think, "You people are so *old*. How can you not notice that?" (You wouldn't say anything, of course, because you were a "good" daughter.)

It is April 1990. My mother is lying in her bed in Evergreen Rehabilitation Hospital with orange juice all over her. My mother lies wearing a urine-soaked diaper in a bed covered in orange juice. She hasn't remembered how to use her left hand yet, and she spilled her plastic juice container trying to pick it up. I've come to visit at the end of another long working day and she is covered in orange juice. "How long has she been lying like this? How long has it been since you checked on her?" I try to sound supportive and calm as I ask the nurse these questions, but I can tell by her expression that I am screaming.

My sisters and I take turns coming to the hospital to feed her dinner. Otherwise, she won't eat anything at all. Night after night the kitchen staff bring her tray of food, placing it on the hospital table parallel to her bed. They don't have time to set up her tray, let alone stay and feed her. They have other patients to attend to, a hundred more meals to deliver. They have no time for a 71-year old woman who is bedbound and cannot speak.

I feel ashamed of her. More than that, I feel ashamed
of myself for feeling this way. Still, I am doing my duty.
I'm doing what I have to do, what I should do. At the
same time, I would give anything not to be doing this.
For those first few days after the aneurysm, my sisters
and I all hoped that she would die. It's what she would
have wanted, we were certain. I would lie in bed after
waking, wishing she was dead. Then shame would kick
in, shame that I could wish my mother dead. Shame
that I didn't love that woman in a flimsy blue hospital
gown, strapped in a chair so that she couldn't fall out.

Though I'm tempted to omit this section lest it scare you off or to
encourage you to keep such feelings and thoughts to yourself, I
know it won't work. These feelings of shame and guilt are common
among people who are caring for their elderly parents. It doesn't
mean we're bad people. Above all, it doesn't mean we don't love
our parents.

It means we miss them terribly and we are desperately afraid
of what is happening to them, and perhaps—even more—of
becoming like them ourselves.

After my mother's aneurysm, I almost never talked about her.
Each time I visited her, I felt that same shame and disgust, coupled with a deep sense of loss. Small wonder I visited as little as
possible.

My father, who had declared "I can't keep her here"—meaning
their home—following my mother's aneurysm, remained active,
healthy, and sharp as a tack until into his nineties. He delivered a
45-minute speech at his ninetieth birthday gathering using only
a few notes scribbled on the back of a greeting card. At 92, he
was still curling, attending meetings, and going downtown to the

theatre. Only when he was diagnosed with Myelodysplastic Syndrome did he begin to slow down. At 93 he reluctantly accepted the help of caregivers in his home. And finally, after several heart attacks and countless transfusions, he died at the age of 94, in his own bed in his own home.

Though his illness meant that eventually he needed assistance for his basic needs, still he never wore a diaper (something that was particularly important to him, since my mother had required them following her aneurysm), was never bedridden (until the final day) and never needed to be fed. He remained articulate and fully aware of his surroundings until the day before he died.

However, that doesn't mean that it was easy to be with him through his two-year journey to death.

"I wish someone would just tell me how this ends," I would often think, frustrated with the demands and unpredictability of my life.

I knew, of course, that it would end in his death. But I wanted to know what the chapters between now and then might contain and what that might mean for me. Should I take the summer off to be with him? Find someone to cover my teaching? What was it going to look like? The fact is that there is no timetable, no month-by-month "what to expect" guide through aging to the end of life. Everyone's experience is different.

Of course we don't want to submit our parents to any more misery than they are already experiencing, but the squeeze we're caught in—between elderly parents, work, and children still at home—does make us long for a simpler, calmer life. And sometimes, speeding things up seems to be the only way to achieve that life.

It's perfectly normal to have these thoughts. It doesn't mean you're a bad daughter or son, or that you're about to commit matricide or patricide. It doesn't mean you lack the compassion gene.

Admitting to these thoughts—to yourself, your partner, or to a trusted friend, counsellor, or life coach—can be the first step towards acknowledging and accepting how difficult this journey is and seeking help for your parents and yourself.

Wishing for the end can happen whether you're living far away or in the same house as your elderly parent. And although your primary desire may be an end to their suffering, a desire for the end to the disruption to your life, and to your constant worry and exhaustion, is seldom far behind. Finding yourself thinking about acting on these thoughts, however, is cause for concern.

If you find yourself avoiding visits to your parents, taking out your frustration through angry words or actions, or punishing them by withholding food or other necessities, it is definitely time to seek help, both for your parents and yourself. Search out a counsellor or life coach who specializes in dealing with aging parents. Talk to them about your feelings and concerns. (For specific suggestions on caring for yourself and seeking help, see chapter 6.)

If you are reading this book, it's because you're longing for an alternative to pretending everything is fine, running away, or wishing for a hasty end to the situation.

Emma, a recently retired woman in her 60s, had been caring for her elderly mother (Frances) for many years. Though they never lived together, their apartments were across the street from one another, and they routinely ate supper together. When Frances suffered a minor stroke, Emma resolved that it was time to move her into a care facility. While her mother recovered at a rehabilitation center, Emma visited half a dozen long-term care facilities that they would be able to afford. She knew that none of them would be up to her mother's high standards, but there were few options within their budget.

Frances had always been a difficult and demanding woman, routinely finding fault with her only daughter's wardrobe, lifestyle, social activities—even her hairstyle. Emma had adopted a style of avoidance and passive resistance with her mother, since direct confrontation only escalated the situation.

When the day came for Frances to move from rehab to the long-term care facility, Emma persuaded her that it was a temporary situation, until she was "on her feet again." Emma knew, of course, that her mother would never return to her apartment, but she left it untouched, lest Frances berate her or accuse her of elder abuse.

As she had predicted, her mother found fault with every aspect of her new surroundings. And she took out her frustration on her daughter during their daily visits. By the time I met Emma, she was at her wits' end. "I'm starting to hate her," she confessed. "I wish she would just hurry up and get it over with. But she shows no signs of dying. Even though she's 94!"

Emma had done her best to improve her mother's experience in the facility, hiring a personal care worker to help to take her on daily outings and to provide care that the staff could not. Still, the daily attacks on Emma continued.

"What keeps you showing up there every day?" I asked.

"I'm the only one she has," she responded immediately.

Emma's guilt ran deep, nurtured by a lifetime of emotional and verbal abuse. But it was destroying any possibility of building her own life.

I urged to her take a few days off, leaving her mother's care to the staff and daily support worker. Though she resisted at first, she eventually agreed, planning a weekend trip to Montreal, two hours away.

When she returned, she emailed me. "I felt as if a huge weight had been lifted off my shoulders. I took in a show, and had a great time with my friend. Of course now, I'll pay for it with my mother."

She was right, of course. When she went for her next visit, her mother flew into a rage, accusing her of abandoning her and of rushing her to the grave. The caregiver, witnessing this attack, urged Emma to stop putting up with her mother's abusive treatment.

Over the coming weeks, Emma and I worked out a schedule of visits, slowly cutting back to once a week. She continued to speak with the long-term care staff and the caregiver to ensure that her mother's needs were well taken care of. On my suggestion, she sent cards to her mother instead of making phone calls, since these always ended in conflict. Though her relationship with her mother remained fraught until her death two years later, Emma was able to slowly build a life of her own, without her mother.

Though Emma's situation was particularly charged, as the only child of a controlling mother, such scenes are repeated across the country, as adult children find themselves caring for difficult parents who have no intention of going "gentle into that good night." (Dylan Thomas)

Do not go gentle into that good night.
Rage, rage against the dying of the light.

All well and good when we think about our own end. Not so pleasant when our frail, dependent parent is the one doing the raging!

What is our responsibility towards our parents?

Does the fact that our parents cared for us when we were children require us to reciprocate in exactly the same manner and for as long as they cared for us (or perhaps even longer, given the rising life expectancy of the elderly)? After all, we were dependent children at the time and they had signed up to be parents. We didn't.

Legally

Every Canadian province, except Alberta, and 29 American states plus Puerto Rico still have filial responsibility laws on the books. These laws date back to the Elizabethan Poor Laws (of 1601) and were designed to reduce the number of destitute and abandoned old people living on the streets or in workhouses throughout the country. Today, they are rarely enforced in North America, though the power of the concept of filial responsibility certainly hasn't dissipated. In recent years, there has been renewed interest in these laws, as nursing homes attempt to recoup unpaid medical bills from the children of elderly parents who default on their financial obligations, or who die leaving unpaid bills. For example, courts in Pennsylvania have heard numerous cases where nursing homes have pursued adult children for their parents' debts.

In China, the notion of filial piety, grounded in Confucian beliefs, has meant that children (in particular male children) live with their parents and care for them. As China has become increasingly westernized, however, adult children have increasingly abandoned those beliefs in pursuit of careers and families of their own. In response to this trend, the government enacted legislation on July 1, 2013, which enables parents to sue their children if they fail to visit regularly.

Morally and ethically

Far greater pressure is exerted from a moral, ethical or religious perspective. Those of us raised in the Judeo-Christian tradition well remember the fifth commandment:

"Honour thy father and thy mother that thy days may be long upon the land which the Lord thy God giveth thee." (Exodus 20:12). In modern times, as in the past, this is often interpreted as providing care (either paying for it or giving it).

And then there's guilt

Most of us dread even the thought of being a "bad daughter" or son. A "good daughter" would never complain, refuse a request, or even take a vacation. In short, a good daughter wouldn't dream of having a life!

In the end, it is not really our legal and moral responsibilities or our sense of guilt that drives us to show up for our parents at this stage in their lives. It is a combination of love and compassion and a desire to repay them for all they've done for us throughout our lives. It is also our opportunity to demonstrate to our children the web of respect, love, and responsibility that binds parents and their children (and perhaps inspire them to follow our example when we reach our parents' age!)

The thread running through all this ...

... is loss. It's not necessarily something anyone wants to think about. Far easier to check the to-do list and see how many items we can tick off. Far easier to do chores, to run around like a chicken with its head cut off, than to stare loss in the face. Much as I like to think that I faced loss fearlessly when my sister was dying, I know that I spent a lot of time rustling paper, making phone calls, and running errands.

Only after my sister criticized me for being distracted did I fully pay attention, and even then I tried to justify my behaviour by arguing that all these things had to be done, and I was the only one who could do them.

The truth was, I was the only one who could be her favourite sister, and sit by her side and talk with her before she died.

Like most of you, I wanted to avoid the reality of her dying for as long as I possibly could. Just the thought of the world without her was too much for me to bear—hence the Bloody Mary at lunch and multiple glasses of wine at dinner. If I just drank enough, I wouldn't have to feel this . . . but of course, it didn't really work.

When someone close to you is dying, you can't help but think "this could be me." Especially when that someone is your sister, only three years older than you. If Carol could die, then anyone could die. Including me.

When your parents are aging, you watch these imposing, independent, powerful adults in your life—your first example of what it is to be a grownup and a parent—you watch them shrink, their eyesight and hearing fade, their confidence wane, their bones turn brittle, their organs fail to work the way they used to. You watch them walk with a walker, breathe with the help of oxygen, and stay alive with transfusions, medications, and a host of other treatments.

And when they die, you know that you are next. Somehow, without even noticing, you have become the older generation. The top of the food chain, briefly; the next to go.

"Not me," you say, "I'm healthy, I eat well, I go to the gym, I don't smoke or drink too much. That's not going to be me."

You know that it will. Even if you pretend to yourself that it won't. One day you too will lose everything and everyone you value in life, and you will die.

This is loss. This is the thread running through this book. And through all our lives—whether we choose to admit it or not.

5

Walk a mile in their shoes

Getting old is not for sissies!
—Bette Davis

There can be little doubt that North American culture is obsessed with youth. Whether it's men in midlife exchanging their long-term partner for a trophy wife or the cosmetics industry offering ever more expensive treatments to combat the signs of aging, Bette Davis nailed it when she said that growing old is tough. No doubt struggling to find decent roles with each passing year, and facing breast cancer and multiple strokes, Davis knew first-hand what it meant to suffer the physical, psychological, and social impacts of aging.

In my family, the Arnups were (and are) famous for looking much younger than their age. When we were children, we delighted in going to the "guess your age" booth at the Toronto Exhibition, to see what prize Dad could win for us. Though he never won the much-coveted giant panda bears (I personally doubt that anyone did), he successfully fooled the carny year after year. When my turn as a young adult came along, I too could hoodwink the dealer, winning prizes just like my Dad.

I still love it when people underestimate my age by a decade or more.

But the fact of the matter is, I'm 65. Old enough for the Old Age Pension, and discounts at movie theatres and on public transit. I'm missing my gall bladder, my wisdom teeth, my tonsils, and an incisor. My joints ache and I suspect that I'm shrinking, although I refuse to be measured.

My doctor laughed when I recently told her that I was becoming the senior citizen my daughters will have to take care of. "You're nowhere near that yet," she countered.

And of course I don't feel that I am. I can still drive ten hours to Provincetown each June and September to write. I like to drink wine, I sometimes stay up late, I love to be silly with my granddaughter, and I still know all the words to the folk songs of my youth—and many from my parents' youth as well. And although I occasionally forget someone's name, I can write for hours without taking a break or looking up a word in the dictionary.

For years before an aneurysm robbed her of her voice, my mother would spend the first half-hour or so of my visit to the cottage telling me about all the ailments afflicting my parents, cousins, aunts and uncles. I wished I could stop her but I could never seem to do it without upsetting her.

"Why are you telling me this?" I wanted to scream. "I don't even know half of these people!"

It wasn't until I started writing this book that it dawned on me that these stories represented my mother's world. Her children having left home and her husband still busying himself with work (he didn't have to retire until he was 75, and continued to be involved in legal activities and curling into his 90s), she probably didn't feel that she had much else to talk about. Perhaps more importantly, this wasn't just happening to other people. This was beginning to happen to her. She was getting older. Her parents had died in the 1960s (as had my father's). She and my father were the older generation now. And, like it or not, they were aging.

And so are we.

Aches and pains, fillings falling out, teeth chipping, grey or white hair, thinning hair, poor vision, the necessity of glasses for the first time in my life, liver spots on my hands, tags on my skin, bruises I don't remember getting, joints that ache. Details I forget. Lots of them.

It scares me. I try to deny it. Sometimes I obsess on it.

A few months ago, Joanne shared a story that epitomizes the experience of aging and the sense of powerlessness that can accompany it.

Her mother called her in the morning, as she does most mornings, in a panic Joanne couldn't quite comprehend.

"What's wrong, Mom?" she asked, looking at her watch as she calculated how soon she would be able to get off the phone.

"I went to the grocery store yesterday and they didn't have any Ragu spaghetti sauce. You know the kind I like, without the meat."

"Did you ask someone if they were going to be getting more in?" she asked, trying to sound sympathetic.

"I did, and they said they're not making it any more. What am I going to do?"

Joanne tried to refrain from laughing out loud or shouting, "Buy another brand!"

I'm sure she succeeded, but she laughed long and hard when she recounted the story to me a few days later. "Honestly," she said, "I just couldn't believe she was so upset about her spaghetti sauce being discontinued, when there are hundreds of other brands."

"My Mom was like that too," I recalled. "She used to hoard dozens of certain household products, just in case they stopped carrying them at the store. When we cleaned out the house, we found dozens of cans of the tuna fish she liked, all stacked up on the lazy Susan."

We both got a laugh out of the situation, and "Ragu" has become a sort of shorthand between us when she's holding on to something too tightly.

"Still," I said, "I hate when they discontinue my shampoo or change the ingredients so it doesn't do the same job as before."

"I hate that too," she confessed. "Just not as much as my mother does."

When we get off the phone, I am certain we both silently thank the powers that be that we're not (yet) like our mothers, obsessed with what we think of as petty concerns and worries.

Today I broke a tooth. I have no idea how it happened, but I felt a sharp edge on one of my back teeth after I took a bite of my bagel sandwich. It might be that I just lost a filling. I won't know till I pay a visit to my dentist. It will be my twelfth visit to a dentist this year. And the year is only half done. My fillings are old—all dating from when I was in my early teens, more than 50 years ago. My teeth, of course, are even older. Not meant to last this long. Let alone for the remaining 20 or 30 years I may live.

It's a small indignity. A minor intrusion. Yet I can feel anxiety building. Will I need another implant? How many more might I need, at $5000 each? I will definitely need another job if things continue at this rate. Even with excellent dental benefits I have to pay the whole amount myself.

I remember my mother worrying about her teeth, anticipating an unexpected dental appointment. At the time, busy with children and graduate school, I thought, "She has all the time in the world. And money. What's her problem?" Now I think the same about me. It's not about the time or the money. It's about my body falling apart tooth by tooth, joint by joint.

Not really. Not today. But eventually.

I'm writing about this because there's a good chance your parents are having these thoughts, at least some of the time. And it makes them feel powerless, as if their lives are out of control. As if their bodies have a life of their own. Which of course they do.

When my father was dying—when he needed oxygen all the time, and walked with a walker, and was short of breath and felt tired all the time—his physician said something to me that I've never forgotten:

"People like your father, who were active agents in the world, have a hard time at this stage."

We would do well to remember that phrase as we wonder how our parents can be reduced to worrying about Ragu sauce and what channel the baseball game is on and who's going to win *Who wants to be a millionaire?*

"There but for fortune . . ."

Do you remember the last time you were sick enough to stay home in bed? On the first day or two, you were likely too sick to do anything but sleep, but by the third day you probably felt relief that you were getting some respite, however brief, from work. By the fourth or fifth day, though, you were starting to get cranky.

"I have too much to do to lie around in bed," you might have complained.

"You're such a bad patient," your spouse observed.

If you were sick for a week or more, you started to get cabin fever.

Now imagine that you were going to be like this for the rest of your life. And the only prospect ahead is that you would have less and less independence as time goes on. This exercise gives you some idea of what it would be like to be elderly, confined to home, to a chair in the living room, to bed. Perhaps it also gives a glimpse of the source of your parents' frustration.

In this chapter, I explore some of the antidotes to your own frustration, and offer a set of tools to help you to put yourself in your parents' shoes.

I'll begin with a story about Elizabeth, a woman I cared for at the hospice. A 64-year-old woman with advanced melanoma, she had been bedridden for the past two months, unable to use her leg because the tumor had destroyed most of her kneecap. She was admitted to the residence following three rounds of chemotherapy and intensive doses of radiation, none of which had been effective in stopping the spread of the cancer. A mother of two grown children, and an elementary school teacher until her diagnosis, we had much in common, including the fact that she was dying from the same disease that had taken my sister's life.

When I walked into her room one Monday morning, she waved me over to her bed.

"Do you think you could straighten up my dresser for me?" she asked. "It's a real mess, and it's driving me crazy."

"Oh my God, it's SO not a mess," I countered. "You should see my dresser." I described in elaborate detail the detritus that lived on top of my dresser—everything from the usual deodorant and spray-in conditioner, to Play Dough masterpieces, stray puzzle pieces, and a Hot Wheels car. "This is a dream compared to that. Don't worry about it!"

"It bothers me," she said. "I have to look at it all the time. I'd love it if you could clean it up for me. "

Until she said that, I had been starting to think that she was a bit of a "control freak," wasting her energy over what I perceived to be minor issues. "I bet your house is amazing," I said, realizing how judgemental I had been.

"Not really, but I do like to know where everything is. That way, I don't have to waste time trying to find things. And of course, neither does my husband!"

We both laughed, recognizing the advantage that having a

well-organized partner or parent provides for all the members of the family!

She proceeded to tell me the desired location for each item on her dresser. I followed her instructions to the letter, without complaint.

That episode has stayed with me throughout my years at the hospice and it guided me when I cared for my father when he was dying. I learned that if I approached someone with a "Don't you worry about that. We're happy to do it for you!" attitude, I was likely to face a sullen withdrawal if not outright rebuke.

Not that it was always easy, mind you. Or that I was "perfect" at it.

It took me a while to be patient (and not to snarl or to make a face) when my father told me for the umpteenth time where I should find the money for his shopping errand.

"In the second drawer from the top, on the left hand side of the tall dresser beside my bed, you will find a small buff envelope of the sort you receive your cash in from the bank. Take out two twenties. That should be enough."

I did not tell him that people, by and large, no longer received their cash in a small buff envelope—or that they rarely received their cash from a person at all. My father had never mastered ATMs, his eyesight and age preventing him from even attempting most forms of "modern technology." Besides, why should he use an ATM when he could speak to a real person, who would politely refer to him as Judge Arnup and ask him kindly, "Is there anything else I can do for you today, sir?"

When caring for someone, whether it's a friend or sibling struck by cancer or an elderly person slowly watching their powers decline, it's important to remember that they see themselves as highly competent, well-respected, and dignified human beings. The loss of control they are experiencing is an attack on their personhood, their independence, their dignity. Small wonder my father treated me as if I was an eight-year-old child, as he repeated detailed instructions about how to get to the pharmacy or pick up his dry cleaning.

I had a choice. I could feel offended at what I perceived to be a slight. Or I could recognize that my father (and my sister before him) were losing control over every aspect of their lives. Eventually they would lose everything they loved and valued, all their friends and family, all their possessions and accomplishments, life itself.

What if we could walk in our parents' shoes even for an hour? Imagine what it is like to be bed-bound, unable to get up to brush your own teeth or go to the bathroom. To be unable to remember what you were about to say, or where you have put your all-important medical file. You too would cling to what you had, and snap at others who tried to take the last vestiges of independence away from you, even if it was "for your own good."

The chances are we will never fully understand what the person we are caring for is experiencing or feeling. But we can be compassionate towards them, and try to understand why they are acting as they are.

Hospice volunteering provides me with endless opportunities to learn and practice compassion and empathy. The woman in Room 4, who levels criticism at everyone within range may be a "bitch on wheels." But if I look more closely I can see past her actions to the frightened mother who will leave behind her three children by week's end. Would I act the way she does? I'd like to think I wouldn't be barking orders to my family about what to do with my investments. But I don't really know.

When your parents act in ways that challenge and irritate you in equal measure, it can help to spend some time in self-exploration. Why does their behavior bother you so much? Do you perhaps see yourself in their actions? That wouldn't be surprising since you are their offspring (whether you admit that right now or not). Perhaps your father's slow and deliberate manner of handling everything from paying bills to counting out change for the pizza delivery man's tip arouses fear that one day you too will be like this.

How to be with our elderly parents

Western society is powered by the motor of instrumentalism. How to get from point A to point B as quickly as possible. How to move up the corporate ladder. How to "get things done" as efficiently and quickly as is humanly possible (and then some!) This ethos is what gets us to work longer and longer hours, to stay connected 24/7, to drive ourselves harder and harder. It is also what causes us to experience greater levels of stress than our parents or our grandparents did. In this culture, speed, efficiency, and toughness are the hallmarks of a successful warrior.

When I talk to people about this book, I explain that it's not really a "how to" manual as much as a "how to be" guide to caring for your aging parents. The tools I provide for successful caregiving of elderly parents run counter to this ethos:

- slow down (sometimes even coming to a complete stop!)
- be present (STOP multi-tasking!)
- don't assume you know everything
- ask open-ended questions and wait for a response
- be patient
- show compassion
- accept what is

Slow down

Do you remember singing along with Simon and Garfunkel's light-hearted song about "feelin' groovy"? Just remembering the lyrics makes me move my shoulders and loosen up my body.

It seems like lifetimes ago. If you're anything like me, you can't remember when the switch happened. Your first real job. Your first promotion. First house. First child. By forty, there wasn't much time for feeling groovy. In fact, life felt a whole lot like a Formula One race. Except that we never seem to reach the finish line!

I vividly remember the year I turned 40. I'd had my second child at 38. I was finishing my PhD thesis and teaching part-time. In short, life was busy. Compared to having my second child, though, turning 40 seemed like a breeze. That is, until my mother suffered a massive brain aneurysm. Suddenly life was all about hospital visits, family meetings, and life and death decisions.

Lists seemed to fill entire notebooks, with barely an item ever checked off. Though the circumstances screamed out for me to slow down, still I found myself swimming faster and faster—just to keep from drowning.

It seemed like the only thing to do, and yet, of course, it wasn't working. Quite the opposite.

Our fast-paced, technological culture has ramped up the speed at which we perform virtually every action. Sometimes it's framed in the interest of the environment (the five minute shower), sometimes our health (high intensity workouts). More often, the need for efficiency and higher and higher levels of productivity push us to do things with a minimum of "down time."

When someone we love is ill, or elderly and dying, the pace and unpredictable nature of events (and outcomes) can drive us almost crazy as it clashes directly with our culture's approach to life.

Dying time

For almost two years, I've been telling people that my father is dying. I spent last summer on high alert, cell phone beside my pillow at night. "He won't live till Labour Day," his doctor predicted, a year ago. Perhaps she meant this year. Or 2010. Last year I took the summer off to care for him. When he didn't die, I went back to work, warning my students that I would have to leave suddenly when my father died. Not a single missed class all year. In April he nearly died—fell in his apartment, stopped breathing, and then revived, despite a DNR order. We cancel appointments, plans, meetings. Gather round. Prepare a eulogy. Make arrangements at the funeral home. My daughter tells her teachers: "My grandfather is dying." Her teachers make allowances. Extend deadlines. After two weeks, they begin to wonder. "They think I'm making it up," she tells me. Crying wolf.

I had to learn to walk slowly in my father's world. But how?

Be present

When you arrive to visit your parents, take the time to get settled. It might help to take a few deep intentional breaths before you open the door to their house or apartment. Once inside, resist the urge to start blathering on and on just to fill the void, or to cover up your discomfort or nervousness.

Listen. Observe. How does the house or apartment look? What changes do you notice since your last visit? Is your father wearing clothes with obvious stains? Are there a week's worth of papers stacked up beside his chair? What might this mean? Is it typical? Might it be a hazard?

Because of our discomfort, we often fall into the habit of cleaning up, putting things "back in their place," or throwing things out that we consider to be garbage or recycling. These actions are likely to cause unnecessary frustration and confusion for your parents. They know where everything is *now*, and you're only disrupting that order.

Sometimes it's hard to remember that it's their home, not

yours. I'm not suggesting you ignore signs of distress or mental confusion. But you would do well to respect the fact that you're still a visitor in someone else's home.

When I was visiting my father, I used to sit down on the loveseat next to his chair, set down my bag, and start drinking the Starbucks coffee I'd bought on the way. Usually I'd ask him an open-ended question like "How are you doing?" and then take the time to listen to his response.

It's fine if you both sit in silence for a while. Nothing bad will happen. Chances are your parent enjoys just having you there, even if he doesn't seem to notice or drops off to sleep. (Yes, this used to drive me wild!) Bring a book to read or a pad of paper to make lists.

Though it made me crazy when my father watched TV (turned up loud because he was nearly deaf and frequently "forgot" to wear his hearing aids) near the end of his life, barely seeming to notice that I was there, still I knew that he appreciated my coming to see him. I won't say that I enjoyed watching curling or golf—it was like watching paint dry, as my father used to say about getting his blood transfusions! Still, now, when I'm at a bar and golf or curling comes on the TV, I find myself watching, as if somehow honouring my Dad.

Stop multi-tasking

Increasingly, neurological research demonstrates that the much-vaunted practice of multi-tasking is, in fact, a bust. Our brains, it seems, are not equipped to do more than one thing at a time, especially if focus is required. The good news is that being with aging parents demands that we slow down and stop multi-tasking in order to be with our parents where they are.

"I don't do that with my parents," you may be protesting. "When I come for a visit, I'm really present."

Are you? Maybe, but I'm willing to bet that you check your

email stealthily on your Smart Phone (or not so stealthily) while your father is reporting his latest symptoms or your mother is telling you about a fall she had while standing on the counter to reach the top shelf in the kitchen. We have all done this, and missed the importance of the story and the essential details.

No to drive-by visits

After my partner's parents moved to Vermont to be closer to her, she developed the habit of adding two or three drive-by visits to their condo into her weekly routine. She would listen to their stories (briefly) and pick up the list of chores they needed her to perform.

While she assured me that they enjoyed these visits, I wasn't so sure. I knew that I didn't like it when she made what amounted to drive-by phone calls to me. (You know what I mean—the sort of activities you engage in so you can check things off on your to-do list!) I knew that my father always took some time to get comfortable with my presence before he would tell the stories he had saved up for me. Because his life moved at a pace much slower than mine, he found the process of my coming and going required an adjustment that was hardly worth the effort if I just raced in and out.

Find ways to engage

When my father was dying, my eldest sister used to ask me, "What do you do all day when you visit Dad?" She found herself bored and uncomfortable after just a few minutes, wanting to get up and do something, or even head back on the road. I will admit I often felt that way with my mother, who was not able to carry on much of a conversation because of her aphasia. Even then I knew instinctively that, if I didn't slow down, I would only frustrate her as I'd begin completing her sentences before she had a chance to say them.

51

Whether it's because of poor hearing, weak eyesight, cognitive damage, or other health issue, elderly parents move more slowly. If you are to have enjoyable and meaningful visits with your parents, you need to dial it back to their speed.

Find ways to engage with your parents. Perhaps you could watch a television show or a DVD together. If you can bring yourself to pay attention, you might even enjoy yourself! Looking at old family photograph albums together can give your parents a chance to reminisce and provide you with the opportunity to learn the names of long-deceased relatives, something you won't be able to do after your parents die.

Sometimes asking a question about their early life allows your parent to return to a happier time, when life was just unfolding. Beware, though. Sometimes your parent may become a little confused, as my father did when he asked me if I had been present at his wedding! His question was so disconcerting to me (did it mean he was losing his incredibly sharp mind? Was this the first sign of Alzheimer's?) I had to gather myself together to respond, "No, Dad: I wasn't born yet!"

What really matters

On the phone my partner tells me about a story she has just read. "It snuck up on me," she says. "I wasn't expecting a story about a father's death."

Nancy's father is dying. She and her sister are researching treatments and the trajectories of the illness. My partner's sister is an epidemiologist. She knows about disease. But this is not "disease." This is her father. My partner is a consultant who crunches numbers for socially responsible businesses. She knows about planning. But this is not something she can plan. She makes lists and phone calls, pops by to report her findings to her parents. Her mother is trying her best to pretend that none of this is happening. Charlie sleeps most of the time, except when he is eating.

The father in the story tells his family how he wishes that no one knew that he was dying. He wishes that everyone would act the way they used to, instead of focusing on his death.

I pause. I try not to sound like the Expert on Death.

"The Buddhists would say," I begin, "that the awareness of death sharpens our ability to be fully present. To set aside all the nonessentials and to focus on what really matters."

"Of course," I add, "when Carol was dying I wasn't a Buddhist."

I think back to May 1997, five weeks before Carol died. She was lying in the hospital bed in the big bay window of her living room, unable to get out of bed except to use the commode, a task only possible with someone on each side to support her. She was in constant pain and she vomited every day. We were both terrified of what was to come. I would come to her house to take care of her during the day. But in those final weeks, much of my time seemed to be taken up with making lists and phone calls, filling out endless forms and applications for health insurance coverage as I tried to arrange the nursing care she needed.

One day, while I was checking my lists, Carol sat up suddenly in bed.

"You used to come here to visit me. We would talk and laugh and buy things out of the Sears catalogue and watch bad movies. We used to have fun even though all of this was happening. Now you're always on the phone or shuffling papers. You might as well not be here at all."

53

I was devastated by the accusation, even though I knew that it was true. "I have to talk on the phone," I protested. "I'm organizing your care. I'm doing this for you."

"Well, I hate it," she said. "You might as well do it from home as sit there and disturb the quiet."

I wanted to scream: "Do you think I like being on the phone all the time? Because I don't. I hate it too! But it has to be done."

A few days later, Barb, the caregiver we'd recently hired to help, asked Carol if she'd like to listen to the radio.

Not missing a beat, Carol said, "Or I could just listen to the papers."

She meant my rustling papers of course. I felt as if she'd turned on me, chosen Barb over me. Barb was entirely devoted to her care. Barb never shuffled papers. She never made phone calls. She didn't have to, because I did. But hadn't I been there for months before Barb came along? Wouldn't I be there till the end?

At the end of the day, I packed up all my things and boarded a train to take me home. "That will show her," I seemed to be saying. I felt hurt, angry, and terrified that I might already have lost her love and loyalty.

When I reached home four hours later, the phone's message light was blinking.

"It's Carol. Can you call me right away?"

I held her medical Power of Attorney. More importantly, I was her best friend and she was mine. I called her.

"What's up?" I said, trying not to sound hurt or angry.

"They want me to have a transfusion. They think

part of why I'm so weak is because my hemoglobin levels are low. Do you think I should?"

"I guess it can't hurt. How do you feel about it?"

"I'm scared. And I'm so tired. It means going to the hospital again. Would you come down to be with me?"

I hesitated. "I thought you were mad at me."

"I wasn't really mad at you," she cried. "I was just frustrated!"

"You seemed to hate me. I'm doing the best I can, you know."

"I know." She was crying harder now. " I'm just so sick of this."

"I know. Me too. It's so horrible."

We were silent for a long time. Eventually I said, "I think you should have the transfusion. I'll come down first thing Monday morning. I want to be with you."

So often, in a caregiving relationship, the fear and sense of powerlessness can manifest as anger towards the person we love most. Learning to recognize that and forgiving ourselves for our missteps will go a long way towards avoiding misunderstandings and unnecessary battles.

Don't assume you know everything

> In the beginner's mind there are many
> possibilities; in the expert's there are few.
> —Suzuki Roshi

One of the ways people cope with the discomfort and lack of control inherent in dealing with aging and illness is to become an "expert." I reverted to this approach when I was caring for my sister. As an academic trained in and adept at research, I spent my off-duty hours reading dozens of books on dying, researching the merits of palliative radiation, transfusions, and medications for the relief of nausea and constipation (common side-effects of pain medications). I read articles in academic journals at the university and in mainstream newspapers. I hate to think what I would have done had I had access to the internet with its millions of sites (some reputable, many dubious at best), blogs, and message boards. Somehow I felt that, if I learned enough, I could find a solution for Carol's pain and perhaps even a treatment for her cancer.

I sympathize with that younger version of myself. I was terrified of losing my sister, and desperate to find some magic bullet to make things better for her. The problem with this approach was that, in my obsessive researching, I was distracted from simply showing up to be with Carol. (Hence her criticism of my rustling papers.)

I'm not, of course, suggesting that you cloak yourself in ignorance. Rather, I'm urging you to show up at your parents' place ready to listen and learn, rather than to convey (and impose) the latest research findings. Instead of arriving with a bag filled with remedies for dry mouth, hold off until you've determined whether this is still an issue (unless of course they've specifically asked you to bring these supplies)! Ask questions when you arrive. Or simply sit. Get a feel for the room and your parent's state of being before you begin to pronounce on the situation.

Ask open-ended questions and wait for a response
This is one of the most difficult strategies to adopt. Because we feel as if we really don't have time for lengthy visits with our parents, we're often in a hurry to "cut to the chase" when they are telling us stories. When you visit your parents, ask open-ended questions— "How are you feeling?" or "How are you doing today?"—and then

give them time to answer. You might have to ask the same question several times before they get to the heart of the matter. Give them the time they need.

Patience

The strategies I've outlined require enormous patience and forbearance on your part. No doubt you are tired and frustrated and harried and frightened. Patience may be the furthest thing from your mind. And yet, it is essential.

You need patience to enable you to sit quietly and listen to your parents' stories. You need patience so you won't interrupt them when they repeat a story about a doctor's phone call that you've heard a dozen times. And you need patience with yourself when you forget and interrupt or snap at them.

How do you acquire patience?

One practical method I found was to literally sit on my hands. My father had always spoken very slowly and deliberately. This tendency only increased with age. For the first half-hour after I arrived at his apartment, I could hear myself providing speedy conclusions to his sentences. I found, however, that if I sat on my hands, the pain served as a reminder to shut my mouth, look interested, and wait until he had finished his thoughts.

Try meditation.

I'm sure you're laughing at that suggestion. I bet you even said, "I don't have time for meditation!"

Even if you don't have the time or the inclination or willingness to establish a daily meditation practice, you can take the time for a pause, especially when you are with your parents. Before you enter their house or apartment, take three slow, deep, intentional, breaths, allowing yourself to calm down. You can take such a break at any time. When you're in the washroom. On the way from your car to their house. On the bus or subway. Before you answer the phone. After you hang up. It may sound like a waste of time, but try it. I'm betting it will help you not to lose control or get angry. It will also help you to be more compassionate towards both your parents and yourself.

Show Compassion

When we are with a loved one who is ill, aging, or dying, we are in the presence of suffering. It is a challenging, painful experience. No matter how much we wish we could alleviate all their suffering, we can't. We can, however, be open to what they are experiencing and offer our love, kindness, and presence. We can also offer that compassion to ourselves, for this really is one of the most difficult things you will have to do in your lifetime.

Once again, meditation may be of service, because in meditating we learn to sit with difficult, uncomfortable, or challenging experiences.

Acceptance

No matter what we do, we cannot stop our parents from aging, nor can we prevent them from dying. We can do our best to keep them safe and well-cared for (and not add to their worries by being a jerk!) but we can't prevent them from suffering.

Thinking that we are somehow responsible for "saving" them will only frustrate us, leaving us at the end of the day feeling as though we have somehow let them down.

The fact is that most people approach aging, illness and the end of life more or less in the same way that they lived their lives. This is true, despite Hollywood images of death-bed confessions and reunions, of Scrooge-like conversions and the like. Much as I adored my father, he was never going to embrace my help with open arms, especially if it seemed to threaten his independence. Similarly, like many men of his generation, he was not about to talk about his feelings with me or anyone else—except perhaps his minister. "I see no use in that," he told me, when I tried to encourage him to talk about what he felt about dying.

You can't solve your widowed mother's loneliness or change your father's gruff exterior. Trying to do so will only add to your own suffering, and leave you feeling tremendous guilt and regret when they die. Just as you can't keep your parent from dying, you can't change the way things are. According to one of my friends, currently caring for a mother with Alzheimer's, "It is what it is." Learning to accept that will stand you in good stead with all the challenges that lie ahead.

6

Caring for yourself

The irony is not lost on me that, despite the title of this book, when it came to designing the chapter outline, I managed to leave out the chapter on caring for yourself. This was not a minor oversight. Rather it reflects what caregivers so often do when they are focused on caring for someone they love.

Of all the things we believe we don't have time for, "myself" tops the list.

Why do we pay so little attention to ourselves when we are so ready to care for others?

A number of myths surround the notion of self care. Each of these leads us away from attending to ourselves. Here are a few:

- Self care is self-indulgent.
- How could I possibly think about myself when Mom is sick/aging/dying?
- I don't need self care. I just have a drink when I'm feeling stressed (or two or three or four). (Feel free to substitute having a drink with friends, going to the gym, going for a run, playing squash, eating cupcakes. . .)
- I'll take care of myself when I've finished caregiving.

- Self care is too expensive.
- I don't have time for self care! I'm way too busy!

In this chapter, I will counter these myths, providing concrete suggestions for how you can take care of your physical, emotional, and spiritual needs while still caring for your parents.

What does it really mean to take care of yourself?

What would it take for you to start doing that?

I'm willing to bet you've been to at least one conference that ends with a session on "self care." The workshop is usually delivered by a "motivational speaker"—someone who is funny and lively and makes you get up out of your chair and stretch, make faces, and breathe deeply. (I'm with the people who try to remain seated for as long as possible, as I don't enjoy looking like a fool!)

Sometimes this session consists of completing a checklist about your feelings and then another checklist of all the things you are doing to take care of yourself.

The list often looks something like this:

- Are you getting eight hours of sleep per night?
- Are you getting exercise every day?
- Are you are eating properly?
- Are you avoiding the use of drugs or alcohol as coping mechanisms?
- Are you setting aside time to spend with friends and other family members?

For most caregivers, the answer to at least some of these questions is a dismal "no."

There's nothing wrong with the premise of those questions. Taking at least rudimentary care of yourself will mean that you are less likely to get sick, to throw your back out, or to suffer from anxiety or depression. The real challenge is that it *is* very hard to take care of yourself while also caring for someone who clearly requires our care and attention, and whose needs may seem bottomless.

My cautionary tale

One January evening, my sister called and told me that her cancer had returned. The next morning I was in the First Class car on the train to Toronto, 300 miles from my home. It was only 11:30 in the morning, and I was drinking vodka and tonic. Now I never drink before 5:00. You can't drink until the sun goes over the yard arm. It was my father's rule. No matter what the season or weather, at 5:00 o'clock, the sun goes over the yard-arm and you can have a cocktail. Needless to say, there was no yardarm on the train. Just the steward offering me a cocktail.

There are no rules when someone you love is dying. That's what I told myself. I would carry a tiny bottle of vodka in my backpack when I went to my sister's house, where she lay dying in a hospital bed in the living room. At 1:00 p.m. every day, I would make myself a Caesar. Tiny bottle of vodka. Little can of Clamato juice swiped from the First Class lounge in the train station. I would pretend I was drinking tomato juice, a noon hour pick-me-up. If my sister thought otherwise, she never said so.

Sometimes when she was at the hospital, I would go to the ice machine down the hall from her room and fill a Dixie cup with ice. Then I'd pour in vodka and orange juice. I was terrified I'd get caught by the nurses because they might throw me out of the hospital. That never happened.

When she was admitted hurriedly to the hospital

for the last time, I hadn't had time to eat. When she was finally settled in her room, I went downstairs to arrange for a private duty nurse, to tell my father what had happened, and to inform my department that I wouldn't be back for a while. As I stood at the payphone making calls, I poured some vodka into the small container of orange juice I had bought and took a slug. After each sip, I poured in more vodka. I repeated this until all the vodka was gone and all the calls made.

At 6:30 that evening, my sisters picked me up from the hospital to take me to dinner. At the restaurant, we sat down at the table with our menus. The second the waiter left, I looked up at my sisters and fell forward onto the table. I don't remember anything except a feeling of falling onto the softest mattress in the world. I have no idea how long I lay face-down on the table. When I sat up, my sisters were staring at me with dismay.

"What happened to you?" they chorused.

"I don't know."

"You fainted," my younger sister said. "I've been praying all week, 'Lord, take my sister please,' but when you fell onto the table, I wanted to say, "NOT THAT ONE!"

We laughed. It was the first time we'd laughed in a week. Probably longer.

After Carol died, two days later, my younger sister, Carol's friend Marsha, and I drank an entire bottle of wine. It was 10:30 in the morning.

I adopted much of the same strategy when my father was dying eight years later. As I wrote at the time:

Eight years on and I am driving to Toronto again. I am trying to remember which exit to take off Highway 401 to get to my father's apartment. I always get it wrong. That means I'll probably get it wrong again today. It's noon. I left the house at 6:30 in early morning mist. Drove 300 miles in my un-air-conditioned car. I had to stop for a nap, curled up in a ball in the driver's seat, unaware of the curious eyes of other road-weary travellers seeking solace in Tim Horton's coffee and donuts. I find solace in nothing. Except maybe drinking. This is my fourth trip in three weeks since Dad collapsed in his apartment and stopped breathing. He had a DNR order. The caregiver shouldn't have called 911. The firemen shouldn't have resuscitated him. He shouldn't be breathing again. But he is. And I'm coming to visit him, make sure the caregivers are doing their job, and then I'll drive home again.

Before I go to his building, I pull into the mall parking lot. I tell myself I need another lined note pad for making lists and refills for my favourite pen. Right beside the stationary store, Jack Astor's lounge beckons.

"I just want a drink," I tell the hostess. Depending on their mood they may try to seat me in the bar area, a hermetically sealed room where men who look 75 but who are in fact 40 are speeding up the dying process one cigarette at a time.

"I don't smoke," I say, "and I'm asthmatic. Can I sit in the restaurant area?"

She waves to a young man who leads me to a tiny booth along the wall.

"Here OK?" he asks, noncommittally.

"It's great," I say, unpacking my journal and pen from my backpack.

I order my drink of choice: raspberry and lemon vodkas frozen and blended into a slushy and topped with three frozen raspberries. The waiter pours a small vial of raspberry liqueur on top. "Enjoy," he says, in a tone that suggests he finds me vaguely pathetic.

I write frantically for 20 minutes. There is no possible way anyone—including myself—could read my writing. But I never have time to re-read my journal now so that doesn't matter. What matters is the process of writing. What matters is the vodka. What matters is that I don't feel like crying now, though I know I will if I have a second drink, so I decline the waiter's offer of a "refill."

It's been half an hour now. "I'll be there just after noon, Dad," I had told him on the phone, "depending on the traffic." And now it's 12:40. He'll be worried.

At the door to his building—Don Mills Seniors' Residence—"luxurious living for today's seniors"—I pause, waiting for the automatic door to open. At the second door, I wait for the concierge to spot me. I read the sign: "WARNING: anyone with a cold, flu, pneumonia, or respiratory infection, or any of the following signs—fatigue, aches, malaise—is requested not to enter the building."

Each time I read that sign, I laugh.

Fatigue. Do you count nearly falling asleep on the highway?

Malaise. I suffer from malaise every minute of every one of these long days of my father's dying.

The concierge buzzes me in. She smiles when I pass by the desk.

"How are you this afternoon?" she asks. "How was your drive?"

More than my father will ask.

I walk up the carpeted incline past the elevator. Choose the stairs, climbing them two at a time, burning off excess anxiety. Arrive at his door. Apartment 205. "Breathe," I remind myself. I push open the door and I look to my left. My father sits in his glider, watching television. He hasn't heard me enter.

"Hi, Dad," I say, walking up close to him. "I'm here."

"Oh," he says. "I thought you had decided not to come."

"Dad, I would never think of not coming. There was a ton of traffic. It's a holiday weekend, and it took me over five hours to get here." I hope he can't smell vodka on my breath as I lean in to give him a kiss on his cheek.

He nods, before turning back to the television.

He doesn't offer me a cold drink, as he used to when I visited him. He doesn't ask if I'd like some lunch. He doesn't ask how the drive was or how my children are. He doesn't ask how work is or who is in charge in my absence. He doesn't ask if I considered driving my car into the median near Belleville or how I kept myself from doing that. He hardly seems to notice I am here, though I'm sure he would be sad if I weren't. I'm sure he would notice.

I'm not proud of the fact that alcohol became my companion during those caregiving years. And I am definitely not recommending it to you. But as I re-read this piece, written as my father was dying, I feel tremendous compassion for my younger self: someone who struggled to be the best caregiver she could possibly be under what felt like (and probably were) impossible circumstances.

Here's what I'm going to ask of you before I offer the strategies and tools for caring for yourself. I want you to summon up compassion for yourself and the circumstances you are facing. I want you to know that you deserve compassion and kindness and care.

Take an inventory of your feelings

When you first learn that you have a major caregiving responsibility in your life, take some time to determine what you are feeling.

You may feel scared of what is to come, anxious because of your uncertainty, and guilty, either because you hadn't seen it coming or else because you wish it wasn't happening. In fact, you are likely to run the gamut of emotions as you begin to undertake this commitment, including:

- I'm scared of losing you.
- I feel guilty that I'm not doing enough.
- If I tried harder I could save my parents.
- Why did I get stuck with this when my siblings get off scot-free?
- They were miserable parents and I don't owe them anything.
- I'm so sad I'm crying all the time.

It is important to understand what is motivating you before you can even begin to take this work on. Detailing how you are feeling can enable you to bring awareness to your feelings (even the really "bad" or "stupid" ones) and enable you to have compassion for yourself. Then you can begin to think about the choices you have. If you don't recognize that you have choices, you will almost certainly end up feeling angry and resentful—donning a cloak of martyrdom that will isolate you even further from the help you really need. So before you ask for help, figure out how you are feeling (and if you are in need of professional help, get it now!)

Questions to contemplate

What's important to you?

What are your core values?

What would being with your elderly parents look like if you were living in alignment with your values?

What's stopping you from living up to your core values?

How do you want to show up?

Tools for caring for yourself:

- Put the oxygen mask on yourself first.
- Set healthy boundaries.
- Reach out and ask for help.
- If you are feeling anger, resentment, or despair, seek professional help now!
- Take time for yourself.
- Laugh. Often.

Put the oxygen mask on yourself first

That's what the flight attendant tells you during the pre-flight training session.

"In case there is a loss in cabin pressure, oxygen masks will deploy from the ceiling compartment located above you. Please make sure to secure your own mask before assisting others."

This lesson applies equally well to our lives on the ground. As a caregiver, you need to take care of yourself. If you don't, you will probably burn out, get sick, and be unable to care for the person you love. In essence, caring for yourself *is* an essential part of caring for the person you love.

It's not that your parents want to destroy your life, your health, or your happiness. No doubt that's the furthest thing from their minds! But in their fearful state, they often feel helpless and desperate. It's up to you to make sure that you're putting on the oxygen mask, and ensuring your own survival.

Set healthy boundaries

It seems as if everywhere we turn these days someone is talking about "boundary issues." I can't ever remember hearing about these issues as a child, or even as a young adult. No one suggested that my father had boundary issues when he spanked my eldest sister with a hairbrush when she was bad. Indeed, he would no doubt have been praised for establishing appropriate discipline in his highly spirited child.

During the training sessions at the hospice where I volunteer, we spend an entire evening talking about boundaries and engaging in role-playing activities to ensure that we have understood their importance. We are not the patient's new best friend, we are reminded. And we are not part of their inner circle. We are forbidden to bring gifts (including treats from Starbucks or a favourite chocolate bar) or to receive any gifts, however small. We are not to give out our phone numbers or to make contact with patients or their families apart from our hospice shifts.

In this case, the establishment of healthy boundaries protects both volunteers and patients (and their families) from harm. Lack of boundaries can mean that a family member becomes attached to a volunteer, and relies on them even after the death of their loved one. As for gifts, a gift, however small, might suggest that we favoured a particular patient over all the others.

Establishing healthy boundaries becomes much more complicated when we are talking about our own families. The adult child of an alcoholic has no doubt experienced years of inappropriate or nonexistent boundaries, ranging from their drunken parent turning up in their bed to having to find ways to smooth things over, if the parent has left bruised egos and hurt feelings in their wake. Explaining away egregious behaviour can easily become a way of maintaining the peace in the family.

Similar issues can arise for the child of a parent with mental health issues. Children of a depressed parent may be thrust into the role of pseudo-parent at an early age, learning to second-guess their parent's moods and trying to make them feel better. Children with a bipolar parent learn to watch for the signs of a mood shift, and to prepare for the rocky ride ahead.

For such children, boundaries may have been virtually non-existent. How then are they to establish limits as their parents age and approach the end of life?

Even under "normal" conditions, boundaries between adult children and their aging parents can become blurred.

If an elderly parent has lost his or her spouse, or is for some other reason socially isolated, these issues become especially challenging. Only children may find it particularly hard to establish boundaries with their parents. But even if you have siblings, you can't necessarily rely on them to do their part in checking up on parents.

"I know if I don't call her every morning, she won't get up out of bed," one client remarked. "Maybe I shouldn't give in to that, but I really *am* the only person she's got."

When dealing with elderly parents, then, how do you determine what are reasonable limits? How do you establish and uphold these limits? How often is too often for your parent to call or drop by? How frequently should you be expected to call? Daily? Or is a Sunday call sufficient? If you live at a great distance from your parents, how frequently can you be expected to visit?

Establishing reasonable limits—and sticking to them—is a means of both self-protection and, more importantly, self-preservation. Remember, you can't help your parent if you are burned out or sick. Furthermore, if you have healthy boundaries, you can be fully present with your parents and not be afraid of being swallowed up by their issues.

Of course, it's all well and good to talk about boundaries when everything is going well—when both of your parents are healthy and mobile, travelling around and enjoying retirement while you are busy raising your children and building your career. In such times, an annual trip during summer vacation may be sufficient. If you live close by, occasionally popping by their house may feel fine.

But when your mother falls and breaks her ankle (assuming she lives alone), how is she going to manage? Who will come in and look after her, bring her meals, and help with her care? Moving her into your house may be your only option, or at least what feels like the only option. And though perhaps intended as a temporary measure, it may be setting a precedent for future catastrophes.

As I have argued throughout this book, no single approach will fit all situations. Indeed, even within a family, what's reasonable for one child may be completely untenable for another. Each of us has to arrive at realistic limits for ourselves, limits we can live with, limits that enable us to maintain some semblance of our ordinary lives.

Set limits you can live with

If you're a parent, you've probably learned that setting limits and not sticking to them is almost worse than not setting limits at all.

To set reasonable limits, spend some time thinking about and writing down your priorities. Be sure to include work, cooking, eating, sleeping, relaxing—all the things you need to do. If you drive your kids to school or hockey practice make sure to write that down. Then estimate the amount of time each activity takes in any given week.

Now, write down what you think is a reasonable amount of time for you to dedicate to your parents in a given week. Be sure to take note of when you are regularly exceeding that amount of time. Notice which activities are putting you over the limit.

During the second year that my father was dying, I found myself in a time crisis. I assumed it must be a time management issue, and so, off I headed to the nearest Big Box Book Store to get some advice. I picked up the book that appealed most to me—*Time Management from the Inside Out,* by Julie Morgenstern. To my distress, she recommended that I record every single thing I did each day for two weeks. Then I was supposed to notice the categories that these things fell into and total up the number of hours. (You are correct if you guessed that I screamed "I don't have time for this!" when I read this suggestion. . .)

For two weeks running my total reached 225 hours, far in excess of the 168 hours there are in a week. No wonder I was feeling a time crunch! I didn't have a time management issue: I just had too much to do! While the time management book may have reassured me that I was not a poor planner, it did little to help me manage an unmanageable life. Things clearly had gotten out of control!

At this point, it might have been reasonable for me to try to establish some new limits in my life. Perhaps I didn't need to drive my younger daughter to high school every day. As my older daughter pointed out, her sister could take the bus and that would give me back about 35 minutes a day. However, the time we spent in the car was almost the only time we had together, since my father's illness coincided with my new appointment as Department Chair. Our busy lives didn't provide other opportunities for us to chat in the way a car ride provides. Thus this activity stayed on my priority list.

Other aspects of my life revealed similar conundrums. I had already managed to squeeze all my meetings into two days, and my office hours into the times before and after class. I was already a time management machine! The only remaining time slots involved cutting down on sleep (and I did very little of that!), eating (ditto), showering (out of the question), and visiting my father (the source of the time crunch to begin with, and non-negotiable).

My problems aside, I think it is possible to establish some reasonable limits with your children, your partner (if you have one), your siblings, and your elderly parents. (Even work can have limits and no doubt should!)

Talk to your partner or a close friend about your priorities. This way you'll be less likely to lie or to leave things out. What really matters?—and how much time would you like to devote to it? For now, don't worry about whether you have a time deficit. Just make some priorities. Are there things you can drop? Ways in which you could be more efficient? Tasks you could out-source to other people? What about grocery shopping, cooking, meal planning, or cleaning? If you haven't found a way to share those tasks, start now! If your children are old enough, they can each take a night when they are responsible for cooking supper. You have to be prepared to eat Sloppy Joes or tempeh burgers depending on their skills and current dietary limitations but, at this point, that's the least of your worries, as I found when my daughter, her live-in boyfriend, my younger daughter and I shared cooking during my father's illness.) (For additional suggestions, see Chapter 7, "Ask for help.")

With respect to your parents, establish the categories (chores, appointments, activities, help) that need to be done regularly. If you have to travel to visit them, determine how many days a month you're able to travel. Whenever possible, opt for the easiest travel possible. Easiest is rarely the cheapest (e.g. driving is inexpensive, but can be hugely taxing on you). Now is not the time to be frugal. If your parents can afford it, see if they can contribute to your travel costs. Determine what responsibilities you can take on from a distance.

Eventually, this will involve a discussion with your siblings (if you have any), but for now it's a good idea to be clear on what you see as important and what you're able to do. Perhaps you can take a three-day weekend once a month. Think about which of your parents' tasks you can take on during that trip. If possible, include a business day so you can accompany them to a doctor's appointment or a visit to the bank. You'll be in a much better position to negotiate with your siblings and parents if you have a clear idea what you can give without going crazy!

Emergencies will arise. That's an unavoidable part of caring for aging parents. But if you are able to manage your time between emergencies in such a way that you are not routinely overwhelmed, you will be in a much better position to tackle the additional responsibilities an emergency entails.

Follow the axioms

Let's revisit the questions I posed at the beginning of this chapter.
*   Are you getting eight hours sleep per night?
*   Are you getting exercise every day?
*   Are you are eating properly?
*   Are you avoiding the use of drugs or alcohol as coping mechanisms?
*   Are you setting aside time to spend with friends and other family members?

Having healthy boundaries with your parents will enable you to find the time for these essential components of health and well-being.

There are many books available to provide advice and tips on all of these items. As I pointed out at the beginning of this chapter, implementing a plan of action for caring for yourself can be extremely difficult when you are caring for someone you love. Even if you have come to the conclusion that you need more sleep, exercise and so on, finding the time, energy, and willpower to attain these may seem next to impossible.

As someone who avoided exercise for years, I found that once I finally started exercising (in my case running) in my early fifties I couldn't believe the difference it made in my energy levels, disposition, and general well-being (not to mention the endorphins running activates—your body's "happy pills!") When I was visiting my father to care for him, my running practice was already well-established. I would get up early, put on my running gear, and run around the track at the high school opposite his building, all before he had woken up. It helped me to slow down, to settle my breathing, and to let go of some of the worries I had.

Exercising makes you hungry—which helps with eating regularly. (It's up to you to do it healthily!) It also helps you sleep and calms your mind. And it's hard to run if you've had too much to drink the night before, so you may even cut down on or avoid drinking altogether.

In the next chapter, I will address what is arguably the most important means of caring for yourself: asking for (and with luck receiving!) help.

7

Ask for help

The single most important step that you can take with regard to caring for your parents and yourself is to ask for help. However, this goes against the ethos of our times.

Western culture—and American culture in particular—places tremendous value on autonomy and independence, on both an individual and a national level. Freedom from unnecessary government intervention in the lives of individuals and the sanctity of the family have been among the hallmarks of American life since the War of Independence. It is not surprising, then, that our culture has a horror of dependence of almost any kind. (We are comfortable with our children's dependency, as long as they are going to grow up to be healthy and fully independent adults. We view with disdain the "boomerang" generation who move back into their parents' homes following university, divorce, or job loss.)

We pride ourselves on self-sufficiency and independence in that "I can take care of myself" way. As a result, when faced with an overwhelming task like caring for elderly parents, most people reject help when it is offered. "No thanks, I'm doing fine," tends to be the response when friends or neighbours offer to help, as if somehow we will earn their admiration for our stoic determination to do it all.

One of the most humbling things I learned when caring for my sister was that I couldn't do it all on my own. My sister and I were extremely close. Middle children born three years apart, we had shared a bedroom until we were seven and ten, and had remained close throughout adulthood, seeking one another out at family gatherings, and sharing outings and meals together.

It was natural, then, for me to assume a central role in her caregiving when her cancer returned in 1997. I don't want to make myself out as some sort of hero: I wasn't. I was driven by almost equal amounts of panic and love. It was the panic—and the horrible reality of what was happening—that kept me awake at night, and the love that helped me to understand what my sister needed.

From the start, Carol wanted me with her all the time. When I would get ready to leave at the end of the day, she would beg me to stay a little longer. Though I knew that it wasn't possible, and that we needed to rely on others for her care, there was a part of me that was flattered by her wanting only me. She loved me best! And I was going to rise to the occasion—I would demonstrate that I was deserving of that love.

I suspect that we are all susceptible to those kind of pleas.

There's nothing inherently wrong with being drawn to answer such expressions of love and need. Except that in truth we can't do it all. We are not superheroes. We get tired, sick, frustrated, bored, angry, resentful. And on top of all that, sometimes we're just not the right person for the job!

You might think I'm contradicting myself, since just two chapters ago I urged you to show up for your parents—fully and mindfully, to be present with them. And now I'm telling you that you can't do it alone? What's going on?

Though it may seem contradictory, I am urging you to care for your parents *and* to care for yourself, by asking for and accepting help.

Action steps

Make a list of all the chores and activities you will need help with

When you first begin to care for your parents, you may not realize everything that you will have trouble getting done, but it is important to get started on this from the beginning. Your parents' (and your) needs will change over time, so keep the list active and visible so that you can update it regularly. This list—which you might want to work on with your partner and children, or with a close friend—will enable you to be specific about what you need when someone else offers to help.

Some suggestions include: picking up groceries, making a meal, walking the dog, picking up someone at the airport, providing a place for a sibling or relative to stay, or providing respite care (e.g. sitting with your parents, taking your parent out for a ride). They can relieve you so that you can go get a massage, get your hair cut, or just go for a walk.

Make a list of all the people you can rely on through this experience

At first this might seem presumptuous because no one has yet come forward to offer help. In fact, they might not even know your parents are in need of assistance. Don't keep this information a secret (though you will of course not provide all the gory details, out of respect for your parents' privacy). Like the list of chores, this list will grow, change, and fluctuate. When I was caring for my sister and my parents, I was often pleasantly surprised by the people who offered me a place to stay, a ride to visit my mother, a dinner out. Of course, I was also disappointed by some people I'd considered to be close friends who seemed to disappear once I was dealing with family caregiving.

Make a chart that matches up the people with the chores and activities

Of course you won't be able to do this right away, but it is worth making a note beside each person's name regarding the chores they might be willing to do. Your parents' neighbours might be happy to shovel their walk in the winter or mow their lawn, at least once in a while. Their friends from church, synagogue or other religious community might be willing to arrange visits to their home to keep them company. Some people would no doubt be happy to drive them to medical appointments. People will have their own suggestions, of course, but people tend to ask "What can I do?" rather than making a specific offer, so you can help them out by telling them what you really need.

Remember that people really do want to help. The adage that it is better to give than to receive is true; by accepting help, you are giving them this opportunity!

To whom can you turn?

Your partner and children

Hopefully, you have a supportive partner as you enter the marathon of caring for elderly parents. Given increasing life expectancy, caring for elderly parents can amount to decades of work, as parents, in-laws, and even step-parents are added to the roster. Furthermore, if the caregiving overlaps with the child-rearing years, as it frequently does, then—even under the best of circumstances—your spouse is probably picking up the slack on the home front, to enable you to care for your parents (or his).

Still, it is important to frame caregiving as a family responsibility. Make times when you can talk on a regular basis about the impact that caring for your parents is having on your lives. The more open you are about your feelings, the more likely it is that your children will respond favourably to requests for help. Of course this means you have to be prepared to listen to their feelings as well. Your children may resent the amount of time you are spending with your parents, and feel that they are being short-changed. Be prepared to make compromises when possible.

If you are contemplating moving one or both of your parents into your home, it is especially important that you talk about the implications with all your family members. If they feel that their needs and contributions are valued and recognized, children can often assume an important role in caregiving. An eight-year-old can spend time reading to a grandparent, or looking at photo albums and sharing stories of their parents' childhoods. A teenager can assume some of the heavy lifting, whether it be pushing a wheelchair on a walk around the neighbourhood, accompanying on a visit to a museum, or fetching groceries from the supermarket.

When my mother moved into my eldest sister's home, my father paid my younger niece to provide care for my mother during the summer. He was able to claim some of the expenses on his income tax, and she had a ready-made summer job. The pair developed a very close bond over the years, and my niece eventually took my mother to Norway, to visit the land where her own father had been born. The prospect of the trip provided the necessary incentive for my mother to do muscle-strengthening exercises, making transfers much easier. Photos from the trip also provided hours of joy for my mother long after the trip was over.

Grandchildren (or even great-grandchildren) often lack the emotional history that can trigger anger and resentment among adult children. Granny's stories of the past can hold great interest for grandchildren, who delight in hearing of their parents' misadventures.

Whether your children will take on such a role depends a great deal on temperament, age, and interests. My younger daughter, who was only eighteen months old when my mother had her brain aneurysm, had no memory of my mother before her illness. She cheerfully shared her toys with my mother, and the photos of them completing puzzles together still bring tears to my eyes. My older daughter, who was nearly eight, had a much more difficult time reconciling this wheelchair-bound, difficult to understand woman with the grandmother she had loved so much. While both girls continued to visit my mother with me, I could well understand why Jesse would avoid contact with my mother, since I shared many of the conflicted feelings that she did, especially in the first years after my mother's aneurysm.

Friends

As I have written about above, friends are often happy to help, especially if there is something specific that they can do. Breaking tasks down into smaller, manageable "bites" makes helping possible, even for your very busy friends.

If any of your friends (or your siblings' friends) have known your parents over a long period of time, they might be happy to visit, especially if they are still at home or in a care home. For people who have lost their own parents some time before, such visits may provide comfort. Even brief visits can break the monotony of your parents' days (especially if widowed), and relieve you of the burden of daily visits.

Some of your parents' friends might also like to visit, though they may need a gentle nudge from you to encourage them. When my father was dying, though still lucid, mobile, and able to receive visitors, my siblings and I arranged for visits from his minister, his lawyer friends, and his brother—all unbeknownst to my father, of course! People from the pastoral care committee of his church— a group he had chaired for many years—returned the favour by visiting him at his home, much to his delight.

How much bigger and more expansive and loving and lovely our world can be, how much more is possible, when we open up to others and let them give to us!

Work

Although your employer is obviously not going to offer to share the caregiving tasks with you, there are myriad ways in which they can accommodate your needs. Once again, think about the ways that a flexible or reduced workload could help you. Many places of employment offer family responsibility days—which can be used for child care or elder care needs. If your employer offers "flex" hours, you may be able to come in earlier or later than usual, or compress your work week into four days. For many people, telecommuting is a practical alternative, at least for a day or two a week. This would allow you to be nearby should your parent need you.

One of my coaching clients was reluctant to ask her supervisor for accommodation when her mother was dying. Since her mother lived in Florida, she needed time off to be able to travel—almost always at the last minute in order to respond to medical crises. "Practically everyone at work is dealing with these issues and they aren't asking for special favours," she told me.

"This isn't about favours," I pointed out. "It's about accommodation."

In some instances (especially in unionized workplaces) employers may have a duty to accommodate an employee's family responsibilities. Even if they don't feel an obligation, they can usually appreciate the impact that your caregiving responsibilities can have on your productivity. Assuming that your employer has put significant time and resources into your career, they will likely recognize your long-term value to the company and provide some form of accommodation.

There may be other forms of support available through your

workplace. Employee Assistance Programs provide a number of free counseling sessions for employees which you can use both for support and to help you strategize other ways to get help.

When my father became ill in 2003, I had just been appointed Director of a department at the university where I taught. I soon found myself needing to travel to Toronto to visit and care for him. I kept on top of my work via email. In those days that meant using the wired computer in the library of the seniors' building where he lived, or alternatively paying $2 for internet access at the computer and video game store in the mall across the street. I often found myself approving grades and writing memos in the midst of a bunch of foul-mouthed twelve year olds who were busy killing one another on screen.

The family doctor

As soon as you have begun to take some responsibility for your parents' care, make an appointment for yourself and your parents with their physician. (Unless your parents have been declared incompetent, you will need their permission in order to talk with their doctor.) Discuss the appointment with your parents beforehand and compile a list of questions with them. You will need to know what medications they are receiving and what side effects, if any, you can anticipate. At the appointment, talk openly about your parents' health. It helps to take notes, so that you can review details with your parents and your siblings after the appointment.

During the two years that my father was dying, he was attended to by a cardiologist and a haematologist, as well as various emergency room doctors. We were fortunate that his primary care doctor (family physician) wanted to take an active role in his care. ("I'm the quarterback," he told us, to my father's delight.) This doctor was a specialist in family medicine, and he did the liaison work between the specialists. This was important because my father revered his doctor and trusted his advice completely.

If possible, establish and maintain such a relationship with your parents' physician early in the caregiving journey. This will be essential when crises inevitably arise.

A word about your parents' perspective

Your parents are ultimately in charge of their own lives. Unless they have been declared incompetent, they are able to accept or refuse any of the services or offers of help you may seek to provide.

Your success in this, as in all matters, depends in part on how you approach this issue with your parents. Bearing in mind that they have the right to refuse (and perhaps knowing that they very likely will, at the beginning), bring them the information, one issue at a time, and talk about why you think this might be a good idea. Then let them sit with it for a time. If you force the issue you are almost certain to meet resistance. If possible, provide information on two or three different services that might address the need so that they can choose which one they prefer.

Of course, no matter how hard you try and how wonderful the service providers may be, it is likely that your parents will at first be reluctant to receive any help from outside of the family. Many elderly people are hesitant to allow "strangers" into their home. Tread slowly and lightly.

The reality is that, despite your parents' resistance or outright refusal to accept outside help, such help will eventually be required. The best thing that you can do is to hold your parents with compassion, while asserting the need for "outside" help. You really *can't* do it all!

Finally, it's important to remember that your parents' needs will change over time, often suddenly, as a result of a fall or other medical emergency. Just when you think you've "got it all under control," the situation will change and you may find yourself reeling. When possible, do your research ahead of the game, before you're in a crisis!

Remember: barring the diagnosis of a terminal illness (and sometimes even then), your parents are likely to live well into their eighties or nineties. You need a long-term strategy, and lots of support and help along the way!

For a list of organizations and services that provide support for caregivers, please see the Resources section on the website.

8

One big happy family

Health care and elder care systems in North America still operate on the assumption that family members (in particular women—wives, mothers, sisters, daughters, daughters-in-law, nieces, granddaughters) will be able to care for ill, injured, aging, and elderly family members once they are discharged from hospital. However, as I documented in Chapter 3, that assumption is far more myth than reality today.

While millions of families do their best to care for their elderly parents, full-time employment, child care responsibilities, geographic separation, and disagreements among siblings present enormous challenges.

Family dynamics in hard times

Media representations often offer images of intact multi-generational families arriving just in time for the final exchanges of meaningful messages at the bedside before the dying person slips peacefully away. These images suggest that everyone will get along, share the work and worry, and be compassionate towards one another when someone in the family is dying. Unfortunately, the reality of the family in the 21st century is frequently quite different.

In the face of a parent's chronic illness or terminal diagnosis, family members who might not have seen one another in years are thrown together in what is arguably the most emotionally charged time of their lives. Not surprisingly, family dynamics, differing perspectives, and past experiences may come to the fore. In debunking the myth of "one big happy family," I am not suggesting that family members are bad, selfish, or even troublesome. These are extremely difficult times, for which nothing in our lives has really prepared us.

Different experiences

Even though siblings may have grown up with the same parents, their upbringing may differ widely. In my own family, my eldest sister, born in 1943, bore the brunt of my parents' inexperience. An exuberant child, she had a "wild streak" appropriate to the stereotype that accompanied her red hair. When she cried between the mandated four-hour feedings, the doctor recommended that my mother let her "cry it out," lest she become spoiled. When she swore for the first time, my mother literally washed her mouth out with soap, a punishment no doubt recommended by her own mother. By the time there were four daughters in the family, my sister had begun tying bed-sheets together so that she could climb out of her room to freedom. Finally, in exasperation, my father escorted her to Ontario Ladies' College—a private girls' boarding school located in a castle about an hour's drive from our house— where she spent the next three-and-a-half years of her life.

By the time my youngest sister arrived, in 1955, Dr. Spock held sway and my mother had learned that affection, hugging, kissing, comforting, and playing with a young child were the avenues to successful childrearing. Needless to say, her childhood was vastly different from my oldest sister's (as were those of the two remaining sisters, Carol and me).

Furthermore, in families where the children actually straddle generations (e.g. my eldest sister, having been born in 1943, missed the women's movement, the anti-war movement, and the counter-culture during which I came of age) the older siblings might well hold beliefs and attitudes more similar to their parents' than to those held by their younger, more "hip" siblings. Their views on everything from gender roles to the duties adult children owed towards their elderly parents might differ dramatically.

In blended families, children (even adult children) may resent the addition of a new parent and new siblings into their lives. Despite the happy world of *The Brady Bunch*—an American sitcom that ran from 1969 to 1974, in which a widow with three girls and a widower with three boys marry and create a family, with hilarious results—the reality of divorce can also include bitter custody and financial disputes, and more.

These differences (and many others) may surface when a parent is sick. As I learned from dealing with my own parents' illness and deaths, my siblings and I became what I like to term "more like ourselves" with each passing crisis-filled year. When my mother was diagnosed with terminal lung cancer shortly after my father's death, the strain was such that each of us retreated to our separate corners. Without the unifying force of my sister Carol, whom everyone adored, and my father, to whom everyone deferred, I began researching palliative care options, my younger sister began researching disease trajectories and treatment options, while my eldest sister dreamed of taking my mother on one last trip to Norway. Nonetheless, we all rallied to ensure that our mother had the care she needed until the end of her life. As my father once said to me, "It's a blessing that we're a family that always pulls together during difficult times."

Not all families are so blessed. And the fact that my father had enough money to pay for his own care and our mother's enabled us to avoid a host of the financial issues and conflicts that plague other families.

Finances

Caring for elderly parents can be an extremely costly affair. If your parents do not have sufficient resources to pay for their care, you and your siblings may find yourselves responsible for costs amounting to tens, and even hundreds, of thousands of dollars. This is particularly true if your parents require one-on-one care.

In Canada, the cost of hospital, hospice, and physicians' services are all covered by government health insurance programs. As well, most of the cost of medications is covered for people aged 65 and over. For those people who have private medical insurance as well, additional services (e.g. physiotherapy, rehabilitation services, medical devices) are available.

In the United States, Medicare covers basic medical services for people aged 65 and over. Nonetheless, health care remains "the biggest expense in retirement—and the hardest to predict." According to a study reported in the *Washington Post* in September 2014, costs such as medical supplies and equipment, in-home care, and taking time off work meant that nearly half of the family caregivers surveyed spent $5000 per year providing care for elderly family members. Some 7% spent over $50,000 or more! A survey conducted for PNC Financial in September 2014 found that one in three respondents who are caring "for their elderly parents spend more than 10 percent of their own retirement savings caring for a loved one."

In both countries, home care services, including personal care workers and licensed practical nurses, are rarely covered by medical insurance. In the five months during which my father required

24/7 care, the cost amounted to $65,000. This did not include his rent or the meals and other services his residence provided. One day when I visited him, he told me, with tears in his eyes, that he couldn't afford it any more. He was concerned that the cost of his care was using up the money he intended to pass on to his daughters. I reassured him that we couldn't afford *not* to have those services, since none of us was in a position to come and care for him. "You're providing us with peace of mind," I told him, "and you can't put a dollar figure on that."

Luckily, my father had sufficient resources to be able to pay for his care. Many elderly people do not. Michelle's mother was diagnosed with Alzheimer's nearly a decade ago. As the disease progressed Michelle and her sister (two of twelve siblings) shared "custody" of their mother, with each being responsible for two weeks a month. When her care became too much for them to manage, Michelle moved her mother into a residence near her home. Though her mother had worked for more than 30 years, her government pensions are still insufficient to cover the cost of her care, so Michelle pays the additional $225 per month herself. (Her eleven siblings rarely visit and provide no financial support.)

Sometimes financial issues become a source of acrimony. Robert told me of the dispute that was ripping apart his family. Because most of his family members lived far away or were otherwise unable to help, his sister became their parents' main caregiver. When their parents decided to buy her a car, two of the brothers objected vehemently to this "favouritism," demanding that a family meeting be held to discuss the situation. This issue arose despite the fact that the primary reason she needed a car was to drive their parents to medical appointments and to shop and provide other necessities for them!

I offered Robert a couple of strategies as he headed off to Boston for the meeting. First, I suggested he try to establish a common ground by reminding everyone why they were gathering together:

"Because we love Mom and Dad and we all want what's best for them." In my work with individual clients and families (including my own), I've learned that reasserting this shared concern can help family members to avoid potentially acrimonious discussions.

I also suggested that he remind everyone that the money his parents spent on the car was theirs, and they were entitled to do whatever they wished with it.

Money can cause people to do strange and nasty things. Adult children can begin to plan how they are going to spend their inheritance long before their parents have died (and sometimes even when they are perfectly well!) We have all read accounts of family squabbles that end up in years of litigation, with most of the money being spent on legal fees, as adult children dispute each other's claims.

Thankfully, most people are not like that. And when they are reminded of their commonality, they are able to come to an agreement to support one another and their parents.

Family history

Money isn't the only issue that can divide families. Many people harbour decades of smouldering resentments. Faced with the illness or death of their parents, they may find this anger bursting forth in unexpected ways, which may be unintelligible to their siblings. ("Daddy always loved you best." "You had it easy." "Mom gave you everything you ever asked for.") Such resentments can, perhaps, be deflected or assuaged, if family members are willing to take responsibility for their own feelings. (For a discussion of these issues see "Take an inventory of your own feelings" in chapter 7.)

During my volunteer work in a residential hospice, I've encountered many families in which one or more children were estranged—or had even been disowned. While I always remind myself that I have no idea what might have led to the estrangement, I'm also grateful that my family always stuck together when the going was tough.

Other challenges

One of the issues families face in caring for elderly parents is that the period during which they require assistance can be lengthy. Often, care for parents falls primarily to one member of the family, whether because of proximity, work, or family status—or simply as the person of last resort. Not surprisingly, resentments can build, as a medical "crisis" of a few weeks' duration turns into years with no end in sight. The primary caregiver's feelings of love and responsibility may turn into a sense of martyrdom, coupled with resistance to suggestions or intervention by less involved family members. ("What do you know about it? I'm the one who takes care of her every day!" or "I've done my stint. It's your turn! They're your parents too!")

In recent years, young people, including children, grandchildren, nieces, and great-nieces have assumed extensive caregiving roles. From cleaning, shopping, and cooking, to driving, attending medical appointments, and "baby-sitting Granny," an increasing number of young, usually unpaid, family carers have been put in the position of picking up the slack in the caregiving schedule. While most assume these responsibilities willingly, some may begin to feel resentment at having to postpone their social, educational, or employment opportunities as they care for a grandparent, while their parents attend to their careers and other family needs.

In blended families, conflict may arise between children and stepchildren as to who is responsible for caregiving, or for taking a leading role at end of life and after the death. Former husbands or wives may wish to visit a dying ex-spouse or ex-in-law, to support their children at this difficult time. I have witnessed scenes of open conflict between feuding family members, as grief and fear unleash pre-existing family tensions. (Mercifully, such conflicts are few and far between!) I have also seen countless examples of ex-spouses stepping forth to care for their former partner at the end of their lives, visiting frequently, bringing food and comfort, without a hint of tension.

Family tensions may be greatly exacerbated by the family's failure to discuss matters of life, death, and finances prior to the "crisis" of end of life. (See chapter 9, "Start the conversation"). Rather than being able to turn to instructions and preferences provided by their parents when they were "of sound mind," offspring and other relatives are sometimes left to fend for themselves, drawing upon memories of conversations that may have taken place years before or perhaps not at all. Where one son is 100% certain that "Mom would never want to suffer like this," another might feel that her religious values necessitated that every effort be taken to keep her alive. To prevent such disagreements (and their potentially disastrous consequences) it is vital that aging parents provide explicit legal instructions regarding their wishes.

Only children

Up to this point, I have spoken as if everyone has siblings to whom he or she can turn when coming to terms with assisting and caring for parents. Of course, many people have grown up as only children, or (after the death of a sibling) may find themselves the only one able to assume caregiving responsibilities.

When my father was dying, a colleague of mine remarked, with a note of bitterness, "at least you're not an only child."

At the time, I wasn't so sure I was the lucky one. "At least you don't have to consult a committee before you take a step," I countered.

Only children do face particular challenges in dealing with their elderly parents. Though there may be nieces, nephews, or others who are willing to help, they have obligations to their own parents. In reality, most (if not all) of the responsibility falls on the only child.

Furthermore, an only child's status often means that their parents are particularly dependent upon them, viewing a visit with much enthusiasm and saving every chore, pain, and crisis for their arrival. While adult children with siblings may face sibling rivalry, family conflict, or worse, the only child requires the services of people external to the family, something elderly parents are often loath to accept. For a brilliant, humorous, and poignant depiction of the challenges of only children, see Roz Chast's graphic memoir, *Can't we talk about something more pleasant?*

For only children, it is all the more important to seek assistance from friends, immediate family, and support services.

Abusive or alcoholic parents

While we might like to think of elderly parents as loving, caring people who are slowly moving into their golden years, blessed by visits from their adoring children and grandchildren, for the survivors of childhood sexual abuse and other forms of abuse, the reality is vastly different. It is estimated that one in three girls and one in six boys have been the victim of childhood sexual abuse. Those figures are likely higher given the under-reporting of sexual abuse. (Note: not all of those children are victims of their parents.) Add to that the proportion of children who have suffered from emotional and physical abuse by a parent and a more complete picture emerges of the number of people who have been affected by abuse at their parents' hands.

Whether the cause is mental illness or alcohol or drug addiction, the impact on the children is equally devastating. How are these adult children to relate to an abusive parent who now needs assistance? Many recovering victims of abuse have long been estranged from their families of origin and may have no desire to re-establish contact (especially given the very real possibility of re-victimization or traumatization through renewed contact with the abuser.)

Alzheimer's and dementia

One of the most challenging aspects of most people living longer is the dramatic increase in the number of people being diagnosed with Alzheimer's and other forms of dementia. Currently, there are approximately 44 million people living with dementia worldwide, with between 60 and 80% suffering from Alzheimer's. Some one in nine Americans over 65 has been diagnosed with Alzheimer's, though many people go undiagnosed, sometimes for years. That number approaches one in three when considering Americans over the age of 85.

Alzheimer's causes problems with memory, thinking, and behaviour. All aspects of the disease worsen over time until eventually the person is unable to communicate, recognize loved ones, or care for herself. There is no known cure, although treatments can ameliorate some of the symptoms, at least in the early stages of the disease.

In the past 20 years, organizations and support for people suffering from Alzheimer's and their families have grown across North America. "Day away" programs can provide much-needed respite for caregivers, who often find themselves on duty 24 hours a day. Alzheimer's takes an enormous financial, emotional, and physical toll on families. While the majority of caregivers are (at least initially) the spouses, they face heartbreaking decisions as their partner's condition inevitably deteriorates.

"The financial toll of Alzheimer's on families rivals the costs to Medicaid. Total Medicaid spending for people with Alzheimer's disease is $37 billion and out-of-pocket spending for individuals with Alzheimer's and other dementias is estimated at $36 billion." Add to that the impact that caring for a person with Alzheimer's has on caregivers and you begin to have a sense of the devastating impact of this disease.

Fortunately, resources for people dealing with Alzheimer's and other forms of dementia have grown exponentially (though the need still far outstrips available resources). All family members need to inform themselves of the implications of their parent's dementia and seek support for themselves for this difficult journey. (See the Resource section on the website for a list of organizations and agencies, as well as for suggested readings.)

Family meetings

Even the most loving of families will inevitably face points of disagreement. Whether it's a financial, medical, interpersonal, or caregiving issue, the odds of resolution are best if you can address any issue quickly before it becomes a major conflict. While email, texting, and instant messaging are efficient tools for conveying information, they lack the subtlety required to deal with the strong emotions that will arise. I have seen countless situations where a simple misunderstanding has quickly escalated into angry words and ultimatums.

This is an extremely upsetting and stressful time for your entire family. Those who live close by may be feeling exhausted and overburdened as your parents' health deteriorates. If the bulk of the caregiving has fallen to one or two people, as so often happens, they may feel taken for granted. At the same time, they may feel that they have the best grasp on your parents' needs and should be able to call the shots. Those who live further afield may be struggling with guilt at being so far away and uncertain what their role should be. And your parents are no doubt frightened (and perhaps embarrassed) by what is happening to them, and, at the same time resentful that their children seem to be taking over their lives.

Each of you needs to bring a large dose of compassion to these gatherings. No doubt you will make mistakes. You may say things you regret. Forgiveness and compassion for yourself, your siblings, and your parents will go a long way towards repairing any minor damage.

If you have not already established a practice of holding family meetings, now is the time to start. If possible, a face-to-face meeting is ideal, as seeing one another's facial expressions and body language can help your family to understand each other more fully. If time, distance, and cost make in-person meetings impossible, video-conferencing with Skype, Google Hangouts, Face Time, or another online tool will enable you to see one another as you talk. Teleconferences are also relatively simple to organize. All of these technologies take a little time to get comfortable with, but they enable you to hold at least some of your family discussions at a distance.

Scheduling family meetings, whether online or in person, can be challenging, as you try to navigate people's schedules, time zones, and busy lives. As someone who has scheduled more than her fair share of family meetings, I can tell you that for a time it was the bane of my existence. Fortunately, online scheduling tools have made it much simpler to synchronize schedules without the need for dozens of emails. Doodle and Google calendar are two of the most popular scheduling tools. Of course, scheduling a family meeting is not just a matter of logistics. People have to be willing to show up! If someone steadfastly refuses to participate, eventually you will need to go ahead without them.

If possible, include your parents in family meetings. You are talking about their lives after all, and holding meetings without them may lead them to feel that their children are conspiring behind their backs. Sometimes it won't be possible for them to participate, whether because of their health or their mental capacity. In that case, be sure to include them in setting the agenda and share the contents of the discussion with them afterwards. Make sure they have had a chance to express their concerns.

In my own family, I adopted the role of organizer, chair, minute taker, and reporter for the family meetings we held when my sister was dying. I'm not sure everyone was happy about that, but I didn't really care. My goal was to do whatever we could to enable my sister to die at home and to keep her as comfortable as possible. That doesn't mean I didn't make mistakes. We held our first meeting while Carol was still in the hospital, as many arrangements had to be made before she could safely come home—arranging for the delivery of a hospital bed, walker, and commode, making schedules for visits, contacting nursing and home care services etc. While the meeting was an efficient way to divide up responsibility for tasks, Carol was furious that we had met without her.

I immediately realized the error. In my desire to protect her from potential conflicts, I had inadvertently excluded her voice from the conversation. After this I promised her that I would tell her whenever we were planning a meeting and would include any issues she wanted to have addressed. I also gave her a copy of the minutes. (I had composed the minutes knowing that she would be reading them. Though this meant that I softened the language concerning her health, it forced me to be much more tactful about any conflicts that had occurred, which was probably a good thing!)

I would certainly not claim that our family meetings were always pleasant or cordial. There were disagreements, sometimes tears, and occasionally angry words and outbursts. But family meetings during both my sister's and my parents' illnesses enabled us to share the burden of care and to arrive at decisions together. And in the end, I think we were all proud of how we had worked together to care for the people we loved.

How did we do that? By starting each meeting by reminding ourselves that we were all there because Carol (later, my mother and father) were dying and we all wanted to do whatever we could. Returning to that fact grounds everyone in the reason you are meeting—not to fight or settle old grievances or prove whom Mom loves best—you are there for them.

Be strategic and specific. What needs to be done and who is going to do it? When? Get commitments and make sure everyone knows what they are supposed to do when the meeting ends. Then document the assignments so you can hold people accountable!

If your family gets together frequently and talks about your parents' needs on a regular basis, you may not need formal meetings. On the other hand, if you and your siblings can rarely agree about anything, you might need to bring in a third party such as a family friend, daughter-in-law, or hospital social worker to guide the meeting.

When my partner's mother suffered a major stroke, Nancy and her sisters all converged at the hospital. As so often happens in a crisis, they were running in separate directions, uncertain of what to do next. I suggested we gather together in the hospital's family lounge. As I had with my own family, I began by reminding us all that we were there because we loved Hannah and that we all wanted to do whatever we could to provide her with the best care possible. Then I guided us through these questions:

- What do we know about her condition?
- What is the prognosis? The extent of the damage?
- What treatments and care options are available?
- How will we decide what option is best?
- How will we keep in touch with one another?
- Who will be on-site (since none of us lived in Vermont)?

As Nancy remembers, I held a mirror up to her family so that they could better understand how they were responding. Because I knew them well and brought that knowledge to the discussion, I could stop each of them if they began to spin out of control. I kept bringing us back to our love for Hannah and our concern for her well-being. The meeting enabled everyone to feel heard and supported, and allowed us to make important decisions about the next steps.

Resolving family conflicts

Even in the midst of family tensions, it's important to rise above old disputes and grievances, whether with your parents or your siblings.

- "Why are they doing this to me?" Recognize that your parents are not doing this to you. In needing your help, they are not punishing you for past misdemeanours or trying to ruin your life. They are old and sick and frightened and they need help. Period.
- While this may feel as if this is happening to you, the people to whom this is really happening are your parents. They are aging, growing weaker, and facing the loss of their independence.
- "It's not fair!" As I used to say to my teenage daughter when she would complain bitterly about how "unjust" it was that she had to empty the dishwasher, "Nobody ever said life was going to be fair." Remember, fairness has nothing to do with the fact that your mother had a stroke, or that your father has a terminal blood disease.
- In the end, this is about your parents—what they need, what they are afraid of, what you can do to help them.
- For you, it's about rising to your best self, not stooping to the lowest common denominator.

The rewards of working together to care for your parents can be great. Having a "joint project" can serve to strengthen the ties between adult children in surprising ways. Sara recalled her recent time spent helping her parents: "There were various crises, one after another; my brothers and I talked things over with my parents many times, and it became a family effort. We haven't pulled together that closely, maybe ever."

9

How to start the conversation (and keep on talking)

Priorities and hard conversations

It used to be that the conversation people tried to avoid was talking about sex with their teenage children. Today, it's talking with your parents about the end of their lives—how they want to live their remaining years, where they'd like to be, what help they might need and how they can get it, and about their deaths—what medical intervention they want, where they would like to die and with whom, what would provide comfort when they are dying.

I'll venture a guess that you'd like to stop reading right now.

I can almost hear you saying:

- My family doesn't talk about that sort of thing.
- My parents are very private. They'd never talk about that stuff.
- Can't I hire someone to do that? Isn't there a service I can call?
- Anyway, it's way too early to talk about that! My parents are just fine! It would only upset them!

As the leaders of the Conversation Project note:

"It's always too soon until it's too late."

I won't suggest for a moment that these conversations are easy. No doubt you will feel awkward and uncomfortable—and so may your parents. For many people in their 80s and 90s, such conversations are unseemly whether because of religious beliefs (the Lord takes care of such matters as life and death), or thanks to a stoicism born of life in the Great Depression and the wars of the 20th century. Some cultures believe that talking about death is bad luck, and may speed up the end unnecessarily. (For a poignant and funny depiction of these difficulties, see Ros Chast's 2014 memoir, *Can't we talk about something more pleasant?)* Your parents may brush you off, saying everything is fine, and there's "no need to tempt fate" (as they knock on wood).

What I'd ask you to imagine is how much more difficult it would be to have this conversation when you're in the middle of a crisis.

Let's say your mother, an energetic and active 68 year old, suddenly suffers a stroke at her apartment. Mercifully the cleaning woman arrives a couple of hours later and finds your mother on the floor. She calls 911 and your mother is transported to the hospital. You get the call and race to find her on a gurney in the Emergency Room. She is confused and her speech is slurred. The attendants are about to take her for a CT scan to help the doctors determine the extent of the damage.

"Does your mother have an advance care directive?" the physician on duty asks you.

"Not that I know of," you answer.

"Do you know what her wishes are?"

You fumble for words. This can't be happening! Your father died suddenly several years ago, and your mother has emerged from her grief to live an independent and happy life. You have no idea what her wishes are. You've never talked about it.

Such scenarios are repeated in emergency rooms across North America every day. Without an advance care directive and a designated power of attorney, families are left to make decisions in the dark.

Not infrequently, an elderly person has no family members nearby, and decisions have to be made via frantic phone calls, as adult children debate who should fly in and what they should do once they get there. Meanwhile, in the absence of instructions, EMTs and physicians must use all possible measures (including CPR, intubation etc.) in order to save the patient's life.

You may have vaguely wondered what might happen in such a circumstance, but you assumed you would have lots of time. In all likelihood, you thought, your parent would be diagnosed with cancer, and you and your siblings would have time to talk then. But life rarely turns out as we think it will. If you haven't begun these conversations already, you need to start now.

Here are some suggestions for opening the door:

- Talk about someone you and your parents are acquainted with who was ill and did not have an advance directive. It's always easier to focus on someone else!
- Talk about your own experience of completing the advance directive forms. (That presumes you have already completed them!)
- Watch a movie or television show that raises the issues of aging, illness, and dying. (That sounds like fun, doesn't it?) See the Resource section on the website for titles.
- Raise the issues of their care needs in a small way rather than trying to talk about everything all at once. (e.g. Do they need a handy man, a cleaning woman, a visiting nurse?)
- Tell your parents that you need their help! (i.e. You're feeling overwhelmed and you feel bad about it, but you need them to take something off your plate in terms of helping them.)

Remember that there will be many conversations, not just one. That way you won't expect the first conversation to deal with everything.

The sooner you start, the easier it will get.

No matter how clear you are, life will likely present you with scenarios you never anticipated. But the more explicit the directions, the easier it will be.

Each family has its own style of communication and set of topics that are more or less taboo. In my own family, my father was the absolute head of the household. We never dared to question his decisions or to ask about personal, financial, or emotional matters. As I mentioned earlier, when my father decided that my eldest sister, a "naughty girl," needed to go away to boarding school, we accepted his decision on complete faith—as, I suspect, did my mother. The very next day he drove off with my sister and her suitcases in tow, while the rest of us remained behind with our mother, knowing that we had better be very good from then on! Thus when my father announced "I can't keep her here," after my mother suffered a massive brain aneurysm, we all took it as gospel, and proceeded to discuss other places where she might live. As you can imagine, I was not in a big hurry to bring up delicate topics like money or end of life care with him!

For many families, talking about concrete matters like wills and powers of attorney provide the best place to start. You may feel more comfortable in that arena as well. Your parents' planned trip to Europe in their 70s might provide an opening for such a discussion, without raising their hackles. (Examples: do you have wills, where are they kept, who is your lawyer, where are your bank accounts, what are the passwords for your online accounts, do you have medical insurance?) All these questions will probably seem rather abstract as they anticipate their trip, and they are less likely to react defensively.

Warning! For many families, that may be the beginning,

middle, and end of the conversation! You are relieved to know the state of their financial and legal affairs, and they're happy that it's over with! It's far from sufficient, however, and you will need to use some of the suggestions above in order to keep the conversation going.

It is important to recognize that you are opening up a dialogue with your parents, one that likely represents a significant shift in your relationship. While you're not trying to usurp your parents' role in managing their affairs, you have made inquiries and raised issues you've probably never broached before. All too often, couples of our parents' age have left all the finances to the man of the household, with the result that the wife knows next to nothing about bill paying, keeping accounts, or even writing a cheque! On many occasions at the hospice, a dying husband has told me of his concerns for his wife because she had never dealt with any of the financial issues during their marriage. In having this conversation with both your parents, you might be affording your mother the opportunity to begin to learn about their finances.

Some families talk easily about personal or emotional issues. Whether because of disposition or experience, they are used to talking about hard topics. Thus your raising issues around their hopes, fears, and future plans may begin relatively easily. Again, use the suggestions above as a starting point, and keep up the momentum.

Key things to remember when talking with your parent:
- Your parent is in charge of their affairs (financial and health) no matter how impractical, wacky, foolhardy, or childish you might think their decisions are (and, for very sound reasons: it's not a simple matter getting them declared incompetent). This is not to say that we have to stand by silently and let them put themselves in harm's way lest we hurt their feelings.
- Despite what you might think—that you are the mature one in this relationship and that you have to initiate every

conversation—surveys indicate that adult parents are much more willing to talk about issues like driving, finances, moving from the family home, or their own care needs than you are! They may actually want to talk about these issues—it might take a load off their shoulders, but they're afraid to upset you!

- Your parents come from a completely different generation, and may have a very different perspective on almost everything. (In my own case, I'm much more open to talking about feelings and about death and dying and care needs than my children are!)

- Most adults in Western culture want to remain independent for as long as possible. We can destroy that independence if we treat them like children, or take their power and authority away.

- No one wants this to be happening—not you, not your parents. No matter how great a problem solver you may be, you can't fix this.

- It is likely that all of you have a lot of feelings and emotions about the issues you are discussing—loss, anticipatory grief, sadness. Acknowledge it. Don't try to make this a purely cut and dried issue. It's not.

- Listen attentively to what your parents have to say. Let there be pauses and silence, without rushing in. This can be extremely difficult, and it is vitally important.

Respect the fact that it is your parents' lives you're talking about, not yours. Don't storm in like a major general announcing all the plans you've made for them. Neither should you gang up with your siblings to present a united front. Not only would it be wholly inappropriate, but it would almost certainly get your parents' backs up and shut down conversation altogether. This is a dialogue between adults, albeit not a simple one, and, no matter what, you need to avoid treating your parents like children.

Whenever possible, talk to both your parents at the same time, especially at the beginning. You can always arrange to have one-on-one conversations at another time. Just like you, they may be loath to reveal certain fears or concerns in front of their spouse. It is likely that this first conversation will lead to lots of discussion between them, and to a not insignificant amount of soul-searching. Give them time to think their way through the questions you are raising.

If your parents are divorced, you will probably need to have separate conversations with each one of them. If either or both has remarried, talk with your parent about whether they would prefer to have these conversations with their current partner present or on their own. In light of the fact that the partner may well hold the power of attorney, it would probably be best to talk with both parties together. All this will depend on your relationship with your parents and their respective partners, however.

If your parents are close to your partner (or perhaps to one of your grown children), it might be a good idea to bring her or him along with you for this initial discussion. In my case, my partner's parents knew that I had been volunteering in a hospice for many years and that I'd cared for my own parents and my sister. While this knowledge made my father-in-law reticent to talk with me (or anyone) about his rapidly deteriorating health, it enabled my mother-in-law to open up about her hopes and concerns at the end of her life.

Remember: your parents get to decide their fate. The major decisions are in their hands, unless or until they are declared legally incompetent to manage their affairs.

Legal matters

Powers of attorney

Creating durable powers of attorney for personal care, and financial agreements with designated agents to make decisions should the need arise, can help families avoid conflicts that may last a lifetime (and lead to the courts, the last place you want to be when dealing with your elderly parents!) Furthermore, in addition to preparing and signing such documents, aging parents need to talk with all of their children (ideally, all together) in order to outline their wishes.

In some families, it may be obvious who should have financial authority to take over their parents' accounts. If a son or daughter is a lawyer and/or an accountant, it may be with everyone's agreement that this person be named executor of the will and perhaps also hold financial power of attorney. (A nurse or doctor may be the best person to hold the medical power of attorney.) Even if one person is so empowered, in an ideal world, all family members should be consulted before any important decision is made.

If the parent wishes to ensure that all family members are consulted, each of the children can be designated. This can create problems, however, if one or more of their offspring is unavailable at the time when a decision must be made. Another option is to designate all the adult children "jointly and severally" meaning that any one (or more) of the children can execute the power of attorney, though it is recommended that they consult one another.

If the parent (or parents) are living with one of the children, or if their care is primarily in the hands of one child, it may be most practical for that adult child to hold the power of attorney. Even in that case, however, discussion among the children is to be encouraged, in order to avoid problems later on.

It may be useful to consult a lawyer or mediator to help family members arrive at appropriate arrangements. As with all aspects of caregiving, the most important piece of advice I can give is to *ask for help!*

Advance health care directives

If your parents express concerns about what kind of care they might receive should they be diagnosed with a terminal illness or suddenly struck down by a stroke, accident, or heart attack, the completion of advance directives can be reassuring. By clearly articulating their wishes and designating someone to be their healthcare proxy should they be unable to make their own decisions, your parents will be in a much stronger position to determine what treatment or care they receive. (Details of such directives vary between countries, states and provinces. Consult your local health authority, your doctor, or your lawyer for assistance. For sample forms, please see the Resources section on the website.)

In recent years, organizations across North America have launched educational campaigns to encourage people to fill out an advance directive, and to designate a person (or persons) to hold your power of attorney in order to act as a substitute decision maker in the event that they are unable to make decisions for themselves. In many cases, the forms ask detailed questions about the types of intervention you would want in the event of a catastrophic accident, injury, or illness. Your answers will assist your substitute decision maker to provide instructions for medical professionals that would be in alignment with your wishes and values.

Misconceptions about Advance Health Care Directives	
Misconception	Reality
I must have an Advance Health Care Directive in order to stop treatment near the end of life.	Treatment can be stopped without an Advance Directive if everyone involved agrees. However, without some kind of Advance Directive, decisions may be more difficult and disputes more likely.
An Advance Directive means "Do not treat."	An Advance Directive can express *both* what you want and what you don't want. Even if you do not want treatment to cure you, you should always be kept reasonably pain-free and comfortable.
If I name a health care proxy, I give up the right to make my own decisions.	Naming a health care proxy or agent does not take away any of your authority. You always have the right, while you are still competent, to override the decision of your proxy or revoke the directive.
I should wait until I am sure about what I want before signing an Advance Directive.	Most of us have some ambivalence about what we would want, because treatment near the end of life can be complicated. Advance Health Care Directives can be changed if/when your wishes or circumstances change.
Advance Directives are only for old people.	Younger adults actually have more at stake, because, if stricken by serious disease or accident, medical technology may keep them alive but insentient for decades. Every person aged 18 or over should prepare a directive.
Used by permission of the American Bar Association	

In the popular media, advance directives are summed up by the letters DNR—an acronym that stands for Do Not Resuscitate. "If I'm brain dead, I don't want any heroic measures!" people will say, having in mind resuscitation by means of electro-shock paddles (think of episodes of *ER* and *Grey's Anatomy*). But the end of life, like life itself, is far more complex. And here's where the need for ongoing conversation comes in.

The Family Caregiver Alliance provides the following list of some of the questions that are addressed by an advance care directive:

- Whom do you want to make decisions for you if you are not able to make your own, on both financial matters and health care decisions? (The same person may not be right for both.)
- What medical treatments and care are acceptable to you? Are there some that you fear?
- Do you wish to be resuscitated if you stop breathing and/or your heart stops?
- Do you want to be hospitalized or stay at home, or somewhere else, if you are seriously or terminally ill?
- How will your care be paid for? Do you have adequate insurance? What might you have overlooked that will be costly at a time when your loved ones are distracted by grieving over your condition or death?
- What actually happens when a person dies? Do you want to know more about what might happen? Will your loved ones be prepared for the decisions they may have to make?

While the questions on the forms may seem straightforward, they raise profound issues about how you want to live your life and even about the meaning of "life" itself.

When I asked my students a few years ago, "Under which conditions would you want someone to 'pull the plug'?" their responses astounded me. You've already met the young hockey player for whom driving topped the list. For others, the determining factor was whether they could live what they considered to be an "independent life." A few, who had had experience with an elderly relative, cited the issues of diapers, incontinence or needing to be fed as key determinants of whether or not they would want to be "put out of their misery."

Although my students' answers provide some much-needed humour on this topic, they also made it obvious that the value of our lives and what we hope for changes dramatically over the course of our lives.

For example, to an 80-year-old woman, the birth of her first great-grandchild might be the event she is staying alive for. Once the baby arrives, she might be quite prepared to let go of life-prolonging treatments and therapies. A young father might long to see his kids graduate from college, and successfully "launched" before his death. For this reason he seeks out whatever life-prolonging treatments are available.

None of us can anticipate what the people we love will want (and not want), no matter how close we are to them. That's why having these discussions is so important—before you're faced with a crisis and a major decision.

If you haven't already completed your own forms—or if they are out of date—you may want to fill them out as your parents are doing theirs. Perhaps some beer or a bottle of wine might lighten up the event. Put on some music, kick back, and explore the questions together. That way you ensure that you get your own forms done, while understanding the concerns that underlie your parents' answers.

Dad and the DNR order

My father balked at such conversations—up until his death at the age of 94. A fiercely independent man who had never been seriously ill until he developed a terminal blood disorder at the age of 92, he refused to accept help in his home, even after suffering two heart attacks. When I attempted to talk to him about the possibility of palliative care, he complained to my older sister that I was trying to "pressure him" into a hospice. When I tried to clarify my intentions, he bluntly stated, "Don't bring it up again."

Although we had persuaded him to sign a DNR order so that we could arrange home visits from the palliative care team, he told the doctor on his first visit that he had never signed such an order. When I showed my father the signed form, he declared, "I have no memory of that."

Sensing my frustration, the doctor asked my father what he thought would happen if he didn't have a DNR order and was taken to the hospital.

"They would try to resuscitate me," he said flatly.

"And what do you think would happen then?"

"Hopefully, I would wake up again."

"You know, Mr. Arnup, the odds of recovery for someone of your age and condition are only about 5%. And even if you did recover, you would likely be much sicker and with a lower level of functioning than you have now."

"I realize that," my father said. "But I might be one of the lucky 5%."

My father was a brilliant man, an eminent lawyer and jurist, who still had "all his marbles" at 94. For most of his life he had been one of the lucky ones. He was used to things going his way.

I would venture to say that most people who make

it to 94 more or less intact see themselves as among the lucky ones, and may be reluctant to sign on the dotted line, or to "give up the ghost."

The palliative doctor was enormously patient with my father. Finally he said, "What do you hope for, Mr. Arnup?"

"I'm not afraid of dying, if that's what you're asking."

"I wasn't, but that's good to know. Is there anything that you are afraid of?"

"I don't want to die in screaming pain," he said, "And I don't want to die alone."

"We can take care of the pain," the doctor said, "And I suspect your daughters will take care of the rest."

This episode illustrates two key points. First, it's not always easy to get a conversation started.

And second, sometimes you need someone outside of the family to get things moving. For us, it was the palliative care doctor—a member of a team of doctors who routinely talk with patients about matters of life and death. It helped that my father was a member of a generation that reveres physicians, holding them in the highest regard and following their instructions to a "T." (I hate to think of what our children will face when we Baby Boomers reach this stage, since we tend to question everything that's put in front of us, routinely asking for a second or third opinion!)

Priorities at all ages and stages

In chapter 4, I raised some of the issues regarding safety and independence. These issues, along with dignity, respect, and comfort, will arise repeatedly until your parents' deaths. In this chapter I revisit the issues of safety and independence, as the terrain has no doubt shifted since their first appearance here.

Living arrangements

Increasingly, public policy and older people's wishes coincide on the question of living arrangements. "Aging in place" has become the new watchword in senior care, and a host of policies and services have been developed to enable elderly people to remain in the family home. As I documented earlier, keeping your parents safe is your number one priority; and this will continue for the rest of their lives.

The family home

One of the best things that my father did for us was to sell his home and move into a two-bedroom apartment in a senior's building. He was 85 years old and, though not looking forward to living in a building "full of old people," he felt it was time.

"I wanted to make the decision so you girls wouldn't have to do it for me," he said, adding that it was becoming more difficult to keep up with the gardening and home maintenance, as he spent five months of the year at the cottage.

Since our parents had moved from the original family home (in the 1970s), they had already divested themselves of many possessions. Since I had never lived in this "new" house (and neither had two of my three sisters), we had much less attachment to it or sense of nostalgia.

For many families, however, this would have been the home where your parents had lived for their entire adult lives: raising their children, watching them leave home. It would have symbolized their independence and autonomy, their identity as homeowners. As a result, many older adults don't come to this decision either easily or entirely on their own. (Of course, this is also the house where you grew up. Maybe your parents have even kept your bedroom more or less intact for when you come "home." Recognize and acknowledge that you too could have strong emotions about selling the house. It might help you to be more patient and compassionate about your parents' reluctance to let go.)

Often the death of one parent precipitates a crisis over the family home. While they were able to manage as a couple (each compensating for the weaknesses of the other), the remaining parent—alone and grieving—often simply cannot manage alone.

The following is an all-too-common scenario. Jennifer was one of three grown children of a close-knit family in Calgary. Every Sunday night she would host her parents and siblings at a family dinner at her home. Her father was a retired military man in his early 80s, in excellent health and still active in the community. Her mother had begun to show the early signs of memory loss and possible dementia, but with her husband's help she was able to manage, and even mask, most of the symptoms. That is, until a catastrophic medical event ended his life over twelve horrific hours. Jennifer's mother, numbed by grief and shock, was, in her children's estimation, unable to care for herself. Supported by her three children and grandchildren in the days following his death, Estelle insisted that she was perfectly capable of staying in the family home on her own. However, as her situation deteriorated, the children were forced to move their mother (against her wishes) into a retirement residence where she could receive care and attention, as well as her meals. Four years later she is managing well, despite having broken her hip twice in the past year. Her family hopes she can remain in the residence until her death.

Barbara's parents, an independent couple in their 80s, live on a farm about an hour's drive from the city where two of their children live. Despite their increasing dependence on their children for drives and chores, they steadfastly refuse to discuss leaving the farm. At the same time, however, they will not consider hiring help from outside of the family. While the situation is stable at the moment, almost anything could tip the balance, especially considering the fact that Barbara's father is showing the signs of early dementia (and no longer drives as a consequence) while her mother has suffered from numerous medical conditions for a number of years. Like many adult children, Barbara and her brother both have demanding lives, with children still at home and jobs that require regular out-of-state travel.

What if your parent refuses to move?

What if every conversation with your parents ends in an angry, "I'm not moving. And you can't make me!"? While you might like to think that your parents are reasonable people willing to be convinced by the wealth of evidence you've presented, moving is a highly emotional issue and may elicit anger, sadness, and no small measure of stubbornness.

If you've followed my advice and started these conversations early, you should be able to give your parents lots of time to mull the decision over. Don't arrive with a brochure and a reservation for a "guest visit" and expect a positive response. You wouldn't want to be told you had to move overnight and neither do they. Make sure they have the opportunity to express their hesitations, to ask questions, and to consider their options.

Ask your parents what really matters to them. For some people, it is proximity to family and friends. For others, it may be a beautiful setting such as a garden or river. Are they interested in activities, outings, and clubs? Do your research so that you are able to answer their questions. A visit to the facility may help to assuage some of their fears, especially if it doesn't have an institutional feeling or the unmistakable smell of a poorly kept nursing home.

It might help if your parents already know people who are living in the residence. Perhaps invite them over for a discussion, if your parents are willing. Combating the fear of the unknown is one of the biggest challenges you face here.

Involve an expert in the process. If you are convinced that your parents are no longer safe where they are living, perhaps their doctor can support you in the conversation. As I've mentioned, people of our parents' generation often defer to their physicians and a gentle (or even firm) suggestion from their doctor can smooth the way.

If you are concerned about your parent's cognitive abilities, perhaps you can schedule an appointment with a memory clinic at the local hospital. There, geriatric specialists can assess your parent's abilities and deficits and, if the results indicate serious memory problems, can provide support for the need to move to a higher level of care.

If financial concerns are a reason for the move, be honest with your parents. Talk to them about what it costs to keep the house going, and what the cost would be for additional help and care in the home. If those costs are clearly above your parents' (and your) ability to pay, they may more easily see the merit of selling their home and moving into a care facility.

Sometimes you have no choice but to present an ultimatum. This is unfortunately what we faced with both my parents. In my father's case, we knew that he was determined to remain in his apartment until his death. Yet, after a series of heart attacks and with increasing weakness and fatigue, he was clearly no longer safe by himself. At first, we arranged for caregivers to check in on him, to help with his medications, and eventually with his bathing and getting ready for bed. Following his most serious health crisis, we arranged for 24-hour care. Though my father certainly did not like having strangers in his home and rarely if ever engaged in conversation with them, he knew that it was the only way he could remain in his apartment. (See the story of my father and the caregivers later in this chapter.)

In my mother's case, the severe disabilities caused by her aneurysm meant that she needed around-the-clock care. When my eldest sister was no longer able to provide that care in her home, after 11 years of doing so, we agreed that Mom would have to move to the respite unit, a small four-bed facility within a senior's building about fifteen minutes from my sister's home. Though my mother had stayed there on a number of occasions, her response upon hearing of the move was one of total refusal. "No, no, no," she said, over and over again, with her head buried in her chest. It was heartbreaking to see her so unhappy and to have to insist that, despite her desire to stay at my sister's, she had to move.

A few weeks after her relocation to the respite unit, my daughters and I drove up for a visit. Both my father and my younger sister had assured me that Mom had settled in very well and seemed happy with the move. Once we had established ourselves in the visiting room, I asked her how she was doing. "I hate it here," she said, clear as a bell despite her aphasia.

"But Mom, Dad said you really liked it!"

"I hate it here," she repeated.

My daughters and I exchanged horrified looks, and I quickly steered the conversation in another direction. I have no idea why my mother had told me of her dislike for the unit, while she had told others that she was happy. Eventually she did seem to enjoy herself, and she took particular delight in controlling the television remote control so that she never had to miss a single Blue Jays' game, one of her favourite pleasures.

Whether you are able to arrive at an amicable decision with relative ease or are, like my sisters and I, forced to deliver an ultimatum, it is still vitally important to honour your parents' feelings and to give them as much control and independence as possible. Let them choose the furniture that they will take with them. A favourite rug or painting can lend an air of home to the new place, along with family photos, gifts from the grandchildren, and their television.

For a parent with advanced Alzheimer's or dementia, it may not be possible for your parent to have any say over the decision. In such a circumstance, it is important to let them express their emotions—whether it be sadness, anger, or despair—rather than challenging them. With time, their anger and sadness may pass, as it did with Jennifer's mother, whose story I recounted earlier in this chapter.

Leaving the family home

Selling the family home may actually signal the beginning of a whole series of moves for your parents. Daphne's parents refused to consider selling the family home in a suburb of Chicago, because of its proximity to the trusted physicians and medical services that Daphne's mother Shirley relied upon. Following a serious health issue, Daphne finally persuaded her parents to move to a condominium near where she lived so she could better help them in emergencies. It soon became apparent that the condominium was really a stopgap measure (because it had stairs and needed outside maintenance etc.). A couple of years later, a vacancy became available in a retirement community nearby, where they could get both meals and cleaning services, as well as meet other people through the various clubs and activities.

Following Daphne's father's death, Shirley continued to live in the apartment they had shared. She was a fiercely independent woman who resisted moving into residential care (the assisted living component of the facility). After a series of medical issues left her exhausted and weak, Shirley moved temporarily to residential care, where she could receive all her meals and be attended to by nursing staff. It soon became apparent to her family that the temporary move needed to be a permanent one, and Daphne was assigned the task of having the following conversation with Shirley:

"How do you feel about staying here in residential care?"

"I don't feel good about it."

"Why, Mom?"

"I don't want to."

"What part don't you feel good about?"

"Stigma," was all she said.

Daphne was taken aback at her clarity. After a moment, she pressed for more of an explanation.

"I've seen the way everyone talks about the people who live in res. care," Shirley explained. "There's a stigma."

"No one really needs to know," Daphne tried. "You can still eat with your friends in the dining room."

That helped.

"And not everyone thinks that there *is* a stigma," Daphne offered.

"Yes they do. You don't know."

For Shirley, this had nothing to do with being petty or stubborn. Instead, it was about pride and dignity.

Options

If your parents are no longer able to live in their home, even with support, an increasing range of options are available:

- Senior apartment building or condominium
- Apartment attached to an assisted living facility, enabling people in independent living to get assistance with light housework and go to meals, or even have meals delivered
- Retirement residence
- Long-term care facility
- Nursing home
- Moving in with you (or with one of your siblings)

To the greatest extent possible, talk about each of these options with your parent or parents. Give them time to think about the decision. Remember that moving represents a huge change in their lives. For some it can seem to be a dramatic representation of their decline. For a widow or widower, this will likely be the first place they have lived without their partner for their entire adult lives.

Show them pictures, brochures, websites, and (if possible) arrange for a visit. Some retirement residences offer a luncheon to people who are interested in their services. Other places offer a trial period in a guest room, so that your parent can get a sense of what it might feel like to live there. In most cases, you're not in a hurry, there's no emergency, so give them time to decide. If there's a waiting list, get their names on several lists so that you will have some choice when the situation becomes more pressing. (In fact, it's a good idea to think about going on waiting lists well before your parents are ready to move, since these lists can be lengthy.)

The tone of the conversation

As mentioned before, we need to imagine what it would be like to be at the receiving end of these conversations, rather than being the one who is stuck delivering the bad news. If we can truly remember this, we are much more likely to adopt a compassionate stance, instead of telling our parents what we might feel that they have to do.

Bring your curiosity to the conversation. Ask them how they are feeling, how they think that they are managing, and what they might be concerned about. This will prove to be much more effective than being combative or authoritarian. I suspect that we adopt an autocratic tone because we are so profoundly uncomfortable with the positions that we find ourselves in. In the end, we feel like some seven-year-old kid speaking to his parents about what they need to do (rather than the other way around as it "should" be. . .)

Also, notice how you are feeling. You're probably a little scared, embarrassed, and definitely sad. You can even share that fact with your parents, telling them how awkward it is for you. Vulnerability is often the most effective way to ensure openness and receptivity in conversations.

Tell your parents you are concerned about their health and safety (because you *love* them) and you want to help them preserve their dignity and independence.

Services and tools

Given the size of the population of elderly people and the exponential growth that has taken place in these numbers over recent decades, many services have developed to provide care and support.

- Emergency alert devices (e.g. Lifeline)
- "Granny cams"
- Skype and other video call services for people who live out of town, far from their parents
- Caregivers whose hours can range from a few visits a week to round-the-clock service (working in shifts or live-in).

Of course the fact that such services are available doesn't mean that your parent will readily accept them.

Lifeline

"As you wish," said my father, when I told him I'd ordered an emergency assistance device called Lifeline. We had talked this over many times already. It was one of a dozen or more geriatric technologies that had become part of my everyday vocabulary. ("I have no memory of that," he would tell me, each time I brought up the topic again.)

My younger sister had found a pamphlet in the mail room of our father's building. "Captive audience," I'd thought the first time I saw the pile of flyers advertising home care, meals on wheels and other seniors' services.

"As you wish."

This was his way of ending the conversation. I knew what it meant. It meant that he would quietly resist, in his own ways.

"You talk to him about it," my sister said. "Here's the pamphlet. He's not safe on his own anymore."

What constitutes safety? I wondered—but didn't ask.

Is he safe living alone in his apartment? Is he safe walking across six lanes of traffic to the mall? Is he safe answering the phone to telemarketers who want to sell him land in Florida or twenty-year life insurance policies?

"We've been thinking this would be a good idea," I told him, proffering the pamphlet.

He took it from my hand, picked up his flashlight and magnifying glass to have a closer look.

"We have pull cords here in the apartment," he said, indicating the white cord near the telephone. "That's more than enough."

"I know, Dad. But what if something happens when you're not near one of the cords?"

He looked at me with impatience.

"Nothing has ever happened."

I reminded him of the day when he fell and had trouble getting up under his own steam.

"But I did manage to get up, didn't I?" he said, a little smugly.

"Why don't you think about it, Dad?" I suggested, knowing that, the next time I raised the subject, he would feign ignorance.

When he finally acquiesced, he opted for the pendant rather than the wristband. On the days he actually wore it, he would tuck the amulet into the pocket of his polo shirt, out of sight.

Caregivers

Most of the time, it doesn't happen all at once. Perhaps if your father or mother has a stroke or a heart attack, you might find yourself suddenly thrown into the adult role. With my father, it happened much more slowly. Tiny decision after tiny decision. What to buy at the store. Which batteries for his flashlight, Duracell or Energizer. Which brand of tomato juice. And then one day I noticed that I was making decisions rather than asking permission. With a father like mine, a legal scholar and judge, an "important man," we asked permission for almost everything long after we really needed to. We feared his disapproval, even more than his wrath.

And yet, increasingly, we had become his guardians, if not his parents.

"My daughters have apparently taken over my life," he said one day. Though I was sitting in front of him, he seemed to be appealing to an invisible audience who might be willing to take up his cause.

He opened his mouth as if to protest, then closed it again. He looked at me with a helplessness that made me want to get up and hug him, though we were not a family given to hugging. It was as if this was the first time he had realized what it meant to be (aging or) dying. And there was no one to be mad at, no one to blame. This was simply his life. What was left of it, he might have said, though he was certainly not ready to give it up. "It beats the alternatives," he used to say, though some days he wasn't so sure.

"Dad," I protested, "it's not that I want to take over. You're very sick."

How could I explain to my father that he was no longer safe in his own apartment, without taking away every last shred of his dignity? How could I explain to him that—despite the fact that he thought of himself as

65—he was 94 and in very poor health? That without his weekly blood transfusions he wouldn't still be sitting in his chair, talking to me?

"Dad," I said, "you can't lock the door. You have to leave it open so the caregivers can come in to check on you and give you your pills."

(That very day, the woman whom we had hired to oversee my father's care had called to say that he had barred the door to the caregiver who'd come to bathe him. Since there were so many different caregivers throughout the day, they relied on the door being open, rather than on having a key. Dad had heard the knocking, had made his way to the door—and then had locked it!)

I added: "You have to let them in, or you can't stay in your apartment by yourself anymore."

"Dad," I said, when he protested. "I don't want to be doing this. This is the hardest thing I've ever had to say to you, but you can't stay here by yourself without help. It's just not safe."

Ensuring that your parents are safe while preserving their dignity and independence is not by any means easy, for you or your parents. I suspect I will go into it kicking and screaming myself! As the adult child, it does mean taking on more and more responsibility for your parents' health and well-being as well as for their affairs. For your parents it means an inevitable loss of independence, mobility and physical capacity, and possibly mental capacity as well. You and your parents both need and deserve enormous compassion and kindness at this difficult transition in your lives.

Making amends

Conversations are not just about logistics. They are also about righting wrongs, building bridges, and making amends. You can't make your parents apologize for ways they may have hurt you or slighted you but you can make amends for the hurtful things you might have done. Or at least, you can try to open the door to that conversation.

With my father, I had many such opportunities, as we spent a great deal of time in his apartment, watching curling on TV or simply sitting.

I had been a royal pain in the ass as a late teenager and into my early twenties. I had dropped out of university after my sophomore year ("to make the revolution"). I hadn't spoken to my father for almost three years after he was appointed to the Ontario Supreme Court and, in consequence, had become a "lackey running dog of the capitalist imperialist pigs."

I thought it was about time to apologize for this and other wrongs, before it was too late.

During a commercial in the curling match, I first broached the topic. Our conversation went like this: "Dad, you remember when I was a hippie and I used to say really obnoxious and politically correct things to you?"

"Yes," he said. "I remember. That was a long time ago."

The commercial break over, he turned back to his television show. For him, there was no need for an apology or further discussion.

Finding the joy

It is painful to watch our parents' health and independence diminish with each new day. It is a struggle to maintain a calm, patient outlook when our lives feel overburdened and crazy.

Yet it's essential that we don't let their situation overwhelm us. Though there will be times when we feel as if we can't go on, there are also moments of pure joy and delight, moments of tremendous meaning and poignancy that remind us of why we are doing all this in the first place.

As I was writing about my father as he was dying, I was surprised by how many such moments existed. As I slowed down to his pace, as I opened myself up to what was actually happening, I was able to let go of my frustration and just be with him. I often kept a pad of paper and pen on the couch beside me when I visited my father. The first page contained my to-do list. But I would often flip to the following page, and scribble down phrases, words, and stories that my father would mention. Since he spoke very slowly—even more slowly, in his 90s—I could actually record many conversations almost verbatim. In other instances, I would take my journal with me to the mall, and over a frozen raspberry twister at Jack Astor's, I would write the story of my latest adventure with my Dad.

On the days when I rushed to my father's apartment, dreading his "I thought you had decided not to come" greeting, I might miss the humor implicit in his instructing me where to find the money for my trip to the mall. Or the irony in his instructions regarding our choice of take-out meals. Or the combination of pathos and love in our efforts to pay his bills together.

These moments become the kinds of memories which sustain us through the grieving process after our parents are gone. These memories will survive far longer than the sting of a sharp word. But we can only see them if we are in the present, not fretting or dwelling on the past, or obsessing about the imagined future.

Sometimes these moments happen when we least expect them.

Each time I visited my father, we began the same way.

"Is there anything you need me to do, Dad?" I would ask. Usually my help involved a shopping trip to the mall. On this particular day, his request was very different.

"I don't think so," he said. And then, a long minute later: "I do have a request that I've been too embarrassed to make."

"Oh," I said, a little taken aback. "What is it?"

"I would like you to cut my toenails. I can't bend over to reach them anymore, and they're getting uncomfortably long."

"Where do you want me to do that?" I asked, trying to hide my unease.

"In the bathroom," he said. "In the middle of the night, when I wasn't sleeping, I amused myself with deciding that I would soak my feet while sitting on the bath seat."

He preceded me to the bathroom, in order to prepare himself. When he called my name, I joined him. I don't think I had ever been in the bathroom at the same time as my father before.

When I walked in, he was sitting on the edge of the bathtub, his feet resting on a large brown towel. His grey cotton pant-legs were rolled up above his knees to reveal dozens of purple and blue bruises on intensely veined thin white legs.

"Do you need anything else, Dad?"

"Bring me a bowl of water. You can use the dishpan under the sink. It's not getting much use these days."

I returned with the square brown plastic dishpan, which I proceeded to fill with warm soapy water. I set it down on the bathmat in front of him.

"Here you go, Dad," I said. "Just like Madge." (The Palmolive woman from TV.) "You're soaking in it," Madge would tell the customers in her upscale salon, the ones who always responded in horror when told that they were soaking their hands in detergent.

"How would you like me to do this, Dad?" I asked when he had finished soaking his feet.

"However you like," he directed. "The nail clippers are there on the sink."

I picked up the set of nail clippers and inspected his foot.

"Where do you want me to start?"

"Your choice."

Some choice, I thought. The big toes were enormous and terrifying. The nails must have been an inch thick and were hard and yellowed despite his efforts at soaking. I wondered how long it had been since he'd had his nails cut. I didn't ask. I chose the baby toe. I began by facing him but soon discovered that the angle was too awkward. I moved my body between his legs, resting one arm on his leg. It felt strangely intimate. I proceeded, toe by toe, cutting and shaping, trying my best not to cut him. Left foot, then right. One toe at a time.

"Well, Dad," I said, moving towards the door to inspect my handiwork. "I think we're done. How do you like them?"

"Perfect," he said. Then, not missing a beat, he added, "Do you paint toenails as well?"

All these years later, I still smile as I remember my father's wry humour, relieving any discomfort I might have felt. It was his own particular, understated humour that I both miss and cherish, all at once.

And some stories are poignant—the fact of his impending death unspoken yet acknowledged.

And this is how we pay bills, my father and I. Upon his instructions, I bring from his study the stack of unpaid bills, his chequebooks, stamps, envelopes, address labels, and a calculator. I place them all on the TV tray (a relic from my childhood) that sits between our chairs. I search discreetly in his garbage can for any bills he might have mistakenly discarded in his initial sorting of the mail. He watches, pretending not to notice what I am doing. It is a game we play, every time we pay the bills.

If he hasn't had a chance to open the envelopes yet, he instructs me to fetch the letter opener from the desk. With a lifetime of experience under his belt, he is much more skilled at opening letters than I am. He opens an envelope marked Revenue Canada and pulls out an official-looking letter. Intrigued, he lifts up his magnifying class from the tray, and shines his flashlight on the paper.

"What is it, Dad?" I ask, resisting the urge to grab it from his hands.

"It's a tax refund," he says. "Five dollars and forty cents." He continues, a note of irony in his voice, "It says, 'for amounts less than $10, a credit is carried over to the following year. Should you choose to dispute this result, call this number.' I'll be found dead before I'll call that number," he concludes.

I do not remind him that he was very nearly found dead only two weeks before. I wish thoughts like that don't enter my mind but they do. I just hand him the next bill.

I write the cheques, record the amounts, and then point to the blank line on the bottom right-hand corner of each cheque: "Here, Dad." He signs his name, in a halting, almost indecipherable, script.

In April, he could still write the addresses on the envelopes himself, but he leaves that to me now. He leaves almost everything to me now.

When he gets to the cable television bill, he says, "On your calculator, multiply that amount by 12." He points to a figure on the bill. "I pay by the year," he explains.

I follow his instructions. "$6.87 times 12. That's $82.44," I say aloud. I wait.

"You think that's unwise?" he asks.

I hesitate. "No, Dad. Optimistic."

He waits.

"It's totally up to you, Dad," I say finally. "It really doesn't matter," knowing of course that nothing in this moment matters more than this decision.

"Make it out for $6.87," he says.

10

GPS for caregivers

At this point, you're probably hoping for a road map detailing the major highways, roads, and streets you'll need to take over the next few years. Unfortunately, caring for an aging parent doesn't follow an orderly or predictable pattern. It is much more likely to be filled with detours and roadblocks than with superhighways.

In fact, no GPS for caregivers has been invented. If it had, once you learned what the destination was, you might well choose to take the longest route possible rather than race towards death.

You are going to need company on this road trip. And several boxes of Kleenex. And plenty of windshield washer fluid. And lots and lots of gas.

And if you think this is hard for you, just imagine being your parent!

Charlie

My partner's father will be 87 in a week. Six months ago he looked to be in his early 80s—a little bent, walking a little warily, but still spry, as they used to say of elderly people. In June, he began to have more difficulty catching his breath. He'd had similar episodes all winter, especially at night, or when he was faced with a stressful event. He took Xanax to reduce his anxiety. Sometimes he took it every day. Perhaps he was taking too much, we speculated among ourselves. Perhaps that's the problem.

And then, suddenly, things began to go downhill. His breathing problems became more frequent. He ended up in the hospital one night, unable to catch his breath. The cardiologist on duty thought he had a leaky valve. Appointments were made, tests ordered. The regular cardiologist at the hospital said his heart was fine, just old: the problem was in his lungs. The pulmonologist said he had pulmonary hypertension, and ordered oxygen. "Don't use it all the time," he said. "Just when you need it."

Within a week, he was using the oxygen all day long. And then he wanted a walker.

"You don't need a walker, Dad," my partner said. "You walk just fine."

"I don't feel fine," he said. "I'm afraid of falling."

Medicare provided him with a walker. The oxygen service brought a portable tank. Still, he fell twice within a month. Once he needed ten stitches to close the wound. He began to sleep much of the day.

All this within three months.

What was happening? What name should we give this? Was he dying?

Only a year before he had still been living in his condominium. Walking up and downstairs a dozen times or more a day. Going out to dinner. He and his wife, four years his junior, had still been fending for themselves:

making their own meals, doing their own grocery shopping most of the time. Sure, they relied on their eldest daughter, living in the same town. And Charlie had been obliged to give up driving, voluntarily, his eyesight and reflexes no longer good enough for him to be behind the wheel. But all in all, they'd been doing well. A year ago he hadn't been sure what all the fuss was about.

Three years ago, give or take a few months, he'd still been living in his own house, the house where he and his wife had raised their three daughters, in the town where he had friends, played bridge, and drove to work every day. He'd known every block, every turn, although some neighbours had of course moved or died, so he'd no longer known all of his neighbours. But the world had still felt like a familiar place. Now he lived in a senior's building, up on a hill, far from anything he might be able to walk to, or might have been able to walk to before he needed a walker.

Never in his life had he imagined that he would live in a senior's building. Never in his life had he imagined himself being a senior. He was healthy, active, agile, not overweight, and neither a drinker nor a smoker. His mind was sharp, always had been. He wasn't old and he was not going to grow old. Now people stared at him on the street, in the restaurant. Waitresses talked so quickly that he couldn't understand them. Frustrated and embarrassed, he would snap back at people: "I don't want to talk about it. . . I don't know what she said. . . Get me out of here!" He wanted to say, "Take me home."

But there was no home any more. No house in Natick. No ranch-style house he'd puttered around for fifty years and more. No tools in the workroom, no car in the driveway he could drive any more. Nothing was familiar. Not even his body, that was breaking down like a car past its prime, one day running like a clock, the next at the side of the road with the hood up, with its disgruntled driver standing beside it, frustrated, frightened, wondering how he would ever get home.

Diagnosis

The quest for a clear diagnosis can become almost an obsession in any effort to try to help your parents. Yet in the case of elderly parents, who are often suffering from multiple comorbidities (meaning other debilitating and complicating conditions), such a quest is often futile.

Many times there will not be a clear diagnosis. Not for lack of trying—you will keep taking your father to specialists, trying to get a firm diagnosis (If we get a diagnosis, then we can do something to treat what's wrong.) You calm yourself down with this maxim, though—as the days, weeks and months go by—you are less and less certain of its veracity.

Some days you think: does it really make sense to keep dragging him off to doctors for one more test, when it's clear that he's going downhill and heading for a crash? But if we don't try to find out what's wrong, aren't we just giving up? There are no right answers to these questions and that fact, perhaps more than any other, can lead to enormous frustration and anger. (Why can't the doctors figure out what's wrong with her? Isn't that their job?) And with hindsight, we may learn just how useless the quest for a diagnosis turned out to be. We can waste the ability to simply be present with our parent, in the search for one disease, one solution, and, in the case of the elderly, it can ultimately seem futile since they have so many conditions—not least of which may be old age itself. Ultimately, there will likely come a time when the diagnosis is irrelevant, and comfort, dignity, and quality of life matter most of all.

Mom

Though my mother suffered a life-threatening brain aneurysm in 1990, she still lived for nearly 17 more years. And ultimately it was lung cancer that took her life on December 27, 2006.

After my father died in October 2005, my mother kept repeating the same phrase over and over: "John was my husband. He was 94 years old and then he died." She was utterly devastated by his death (and perhaps devastated too by our refusal to let her go to Toronto to care for him).

When a routine chest X-ray revealed that our mother had a mass on her lung—just ten days after our father's death—my sisters and I struggled to come to terms with the possibility of another death, so soon after our father's. What could we do? What treatment options were available? What kind of lung cancer was it? What other tests were available?

Eventually we convened a family meeting with her doctor. He patiently explained the type of cancer Mom had, and what would be involved in further testing. "We could do a biopsy of the tumour, but I'm not recommending that. It would involve surgery and in your mother's condition—with her comorbidities—that doesn't make sense, since I don't foresee us pursuing any treatment."

Then he outlined the possible treatments available: major surgery to remove the tumour, and likely the lung with it—or chemotherapy, with all its attendant side effects.

"The fact is," he concluded, "your mother doesn't appear to be suffering at all. So I'd say, let's treat the symptoms if and when they arise, and leave well enough alone."

"She has a very high tolerance for pain," my younger sister countered. "So it's hard to tell if she is suffering."

"Be that as it may," the doctor might have said, though likely that would be my father's choice of words rather than his, "I see no reason to pursue further tests or treatment at this time."

"How long do you think she has?" I asked.

"Six months is my best estimate, though one can never be sure."

My mother, wheelchair-bound and in need of 24-hour care for the past 15 years, lived another twelve months, outwitting her doctor and all our efforts to have her admit she was actually sick. ("How are you feeling, Mom?" "Fine," she would say, almost angrily, as if to say, "stop bothering me with such stupid questions!")

Among the diseases affecting the elderly are the following:
- Chronic obstructive pulmonary disease (COPD)
- Congestive heart failure
- Coronary heart disease
- Cancer (multiple possible locations and outcomes)
- Stroke
- Alzheimer's and other forms of dementia
- Mental illness
- Diabetes and its complications

- Kidney failure
- Auto-immune disorders (e.g. ALS, MS)
- And many if not most elderly people have several conditions at the same time, compounding one another and complicating diagnosis and treatment.

For people in their 80s and 90s, a fall often precipitates more serious medical problems. If your parent already has osteoporosis, something as simple as tripping on a throw rug can lead to a hospital stay, with complex surgery being followed by a possible stay at a rehabilitation facility. And the period of being confined to bed can in fact exacerbate or even cause other problems (like pneumonia), which for the frail elderly can be fatal.

It is not my purpose to detail here every possible medical outcome and condition. In fact, even within specific disease categories, each person's experience is different (and complicated by pre-existing conditions like diabetes, obesity, osteoporosis, chronic bronchitis, high or low blood pressure, anemia, etc.) What I will do in this chapter is to discuss some of the situations you may face, and ways in which you can manage them to the best of your (and your parents') ability.

The medical rollercoaster

The search for a diagnosis is just one aspect of the rollercoaster you are on. I suspect you will experience frustration and anger (especially at the physicians who ought to know what's wrong, considering how much we pay them!) along with anxiety, even depression, and an overwhelming sense of losing control. You are not the driver of this rollercoaster, and neither is your elderly parent (nor, for that matter, is the doctor).

What does the ride look like?

Uncertainty and unpredictability are its hallmarks. Just when you think you have a grasp on the situation and believe you can see a path ahead, something will happen—a reaction to medication, a fall, a revelation—and your "new normal" will rapidly become a thing of the past as you struggle to catch up with your new reality.

How to cope with it?—especially if you're like me and never liked rollercoasters to begin with, preferring to remain on solid ground.

- Involve your parent as much as possible every step of the way in the decision-making process. Listen to them. Don't interrupt. Don't talk down to them from your place of superior knowledge (just because you've been looking up their condition on the internet!)

- Remember that it's their life, not yours. That means, if they want to "give up" (your term, unlikely to be theirs), you owe it to them to hear them out. It's quite likely that they will recognize they are dying long before you are ready to admit it. If there seems to be no effective treatment, and they've had enough, maybe it's time to believe them.

- Do whatever you can to keep things in perspective. This is not a battle. There are no winners and losers. There are no enemies (except perhaps cancer). Try not to "catastrophize" (a therapeutic term for the tendency to leap into worst-case scenarios at the first sign of trouble). The fact is that aging, illness, and dying are normal processes—part of the life cycle of all beings.

- Resist giving in to anger. When you feel rage growing, stop. Take some deep, slow breaths. Go for a walk. Sit in the sun. Talk to your partner, or a friend. Chances are that not far beneath that anger is a deep sense of sadness and loss. You are facing the loss of your parent: someone who may well love you unconditionally and who has been with you for your entire life. That's sad, pure and simple. Let yourself cry. Feel it. It won't completely overwhelm you or prevent you from being of assistance to your parent. Quite the opposite.

- Recognize that your parent may be ill for a long time. In fact, you have no idea how long this may last (which makes real planning almost impossible). Both of my parents far exceeded their doctors' prognoses. In contrast, my sister lived only two months after her diagnosis, not six to eight months, as her doctor had thought. How can you deal with this? The answer is: one moment at a time. Whenever you catch yourself saying something like, "Oh my God, this could go on for years! I can't handle it!" just bring yourself back to the present. What can I do today? What do I need today? What do my parents need right now?

- Don't become so obsessed with getting a diagnosis that you forget to enjoy the time that remains. Ask your parents if they want to see anyone or to travel somewhere. If they say yes, then make these arrangements soon. Take a trip with them and enjoy the time you have left with them.

"The best-laid schemes o' mice and men gang aft agley"

Robert Burns' famous phrase beautifully captures what it's like trying to plan when dealing with elderly parents. For a time, when my father was dying, I had a little yellow sticky note on my computer that read: "Expect the unexpected." It seemed to sum up my life at that time. After a while, though, I wrote a new note which read: "Expect nothing." I figured that way I would never be disappointed.

So what's the point in trying to plan, if you have no idea what's going to happen?

I'm going to tell you that you still have to plan, because without a plan—or at least some options—you're going to wind up in the emergency room frequently, and you're going to endure a great deal of unnecessary heartache and expense. Without a plan you will be doomed to spend the next few years in chaos.

What kind of plan?

First of all, you'll need to be very flexible because, more often than you can imagine, you'll run into times where you have to change what you were going to do at the drop of a hat, to take your Mom to emergency or your Dad to an unexpected medical appointment. (Or maybe both at the same time . . . but, alas, in different hospitals!) Back-up plans will be essential (e.g. who picks up the kids if you have to go to the hospital?)

There are some things you can plan (even if adjustments might have to be made):

- Make sure your own affairs are in good order. Streamline as much as you can in your own life. Switch your bills over to automatic payment from your bank account or credit card. You don't want to forget to pay your taxes in the midst of a family health crisis! Make sure you have unlimited minutes on your cell phone in order to cover lots of unexpected calls. If you need to, call your carrier to negotiate a better plan. Take your car in for a tune-up. Have your furnace and air-conditioning checked, as you usually would. Don't defer routine tasks to a time "when all this is over" because that could be very far in the future.

- If you have children at home, make sure that their affairs are in order too. That means, when February comes around, that you make sure that you enroll them in summer camp and other activities. Don't let things slide! The last thing you need is to have your kids sitting around the house with nothing to do all summer while you're racing between your work and your parents.

- Talk to your employer (early and often—whenever there's a significant change in your situation). Alert them to your family health situation. You won't know immediately what sorts of accommodation you may need, but keeping your employer in the loop will make them more predisposed to be helpful when that time comes (which it will—you just don't know when—and it may be many times, not just one!)

- Now is not the time to take on a huge new file, client or contract at work, if you can help it. I realize that you don't always have a choice, but, if you do, consider saying no, at least until you have a better sense of how things might pan out.

- If you are self-employed, recognize that you will probably be distracted and unable to accomplish as much as you normally can. Let clients know what is going on and make certain that they are agreeable if things get delayed a little. If they are not, find colleagues (or competitors) whose work you respect and trust, and see if they are willing to collaborate or just pick up the slack during this challenging period. At some point, they'll probably be dealing with similar issues themselves, and might need you to return the favour!

- Visit your doctor. If you haven't had a complete physical examination in some time, arrange for one now. Talk to your doctor about your parents' health and the stress you are under. Your doctor can be your ally when you need one (including providing you with a medical note somewhere down the line, if you need time off work.) Numerous studies have documented the adverse impact of prolonged caregiving on caregivers' emotional, physical, and psychological health. Don't neglect your own health and well-being!

These moves should stand you in good stead as you navigate this difficult path.

Couples' needs

The disparity in needs and abilities, especially in couples, can make for huge difficulties in planning and finding appropriate care.

The story of Frank, who lived down the street from me, illustrates this challenge. Frank and his wife were in their late 60s or early 70s when Cathy's memory began to deteriorate. Fortunately, Frank was in great shape and was able to care for her at home. That is, until he fell and broke his ankle. (Note the theme: a fall can precipitate a crisis!)

While Frank was in the hospital, Cathy began to leave the house and wander. One day, she was found by police far from her home, perhaps trying to locate her husband at the hospital. They were then in an immediate and (as it turned out) lifelong crisis, because she was diagnosed with Alzheimer's, and had to be moved into an assisted living facility immediately. Frank decided that they should both move into a long-term care facility, where he continues to care for her as her mind deteriorates rapidly. Without his presence, she would have to be in a locked facility on her own. Their house sits empty, a reminder to us all of the fragility of life.

Dignity and respect

Despite what our culture may suggest, I believe that there are no inherently undignified activities or conditions, only occasions when people are treated with a lack of respect and dignity. In other words, dignity is in the eye of both the giver and the receiver of care.

I'm not naïve. I'm not suggesting that it feels good to have to wear a diaper—and it must feel even worse to consciously have a bowel movement in one. After all, our mothers spent a considerable amount of time toilet training us, and we've spent the rest of our lives making sure we don't slip up. It must go against all those years of training and experience to "let it go" in a diaper.

But my experiences as a hospice volunteer have taught me that the single most important factor in whether or not someone feels a lack of dignity is in how caregivers treat them while they are providing care.

This holds true for bed baths, assistance with showering, and every other form of personal care that might need to be provided.

That said, I'm not suggesting that you need to provide personal care for your parents. Though you may be comfortable with it, particularly if you are a health care provider, it's very likely that your parents would prefer that a relative stranger provide such care, rather than their children. So there's nothing wrong with your not wanting to do it—any more than with your parents refusing to let you. While I feel perfectly comfortable assisting staff at the hospice with bed baths or diaper changing, I changed my mother's diaper only a handful of times, and never had to do this for my father, a fact we were both grateful for, I'm sure.

When Michelle volunteered to care for her mother, she could not have imagined the duties and activities that might be involved. "When I gave my Mom the first shower," she told me, "I figured the only way I could do it was by taking a shower with her. So I helped Mom get undressed and then I got undressed and wrapped myself in a shower curtain." She laughed as she recounted the story. "Pretty soon I got fed up with trying to keep the shower curtain up, so I just got rid of it, and we were both naked together in the shower. After I'd gotten her clean, I helped her out and then I finished showering, and Mom watched me. And that was the end of modesty!"

When I told Michelle that I had rarely changed my mother's diaper, she said, "I do that too. I don't have any problem with it. And neither does Mom." I wondered if the fact that her mother has Alzheimer's and is in so many ways not herself anymore eased this transition for Michelle and her mother.

It is difficult to accept the vagaries of aging, whether it's needing someone to assist you with bathing, or, for some people, needing a wheelchair. My father was extremely reluctant to accept either a walker or a wheelchair. I have always assumed it was because of my mother's situation after her aneurysm: needing a wheelchair, having to wear a diaper etc. Or maybe it was his way of preserving his dignity.

I can still see him sitting in his wheelchair, his cane across his knees, wearing his polo shirt and sports jacket, and, if he was going out, his cap—he had a look of such dignity and detachment, as if this person in the wheelchair wasn't really him, he was still Mr. Justice Arnup, a proud and distinguished gentleman.

Whenever I think about dignity I recall Jacinthe, a very dignified woman in her 70s with beautiful long white hair. A highly independent single woman and a senior policy advisor in the government, Jacinthe had come to the hospice to die. One day she asked me if I could brush her hair for her, as she no longer had the strength. As I brushed, she mused: "When I first came here, I could walk to the washroom by myself. After a while, as I got weaker, I needed a walker, and eventually, a commode beside the bed. Now I have this," she concluded, pointing to the drain from her catheter. She wasn't complaining—merely stating in a matter-of-fact manner, the changes in her condition, all of which had been accepted with enormous dignity and grace.

Comfort and symptom management

Given the wide array of conditions and diseases that aging people face, it is impossible to prescribe the treatments and measures that can provide them with comfort. For some people, a hospital bed may eventually be required to enable frequent repositioning in a manner safe for both the care provider and the patient. For others, a recliner in the living room near the television and the bathroom may be an ideal location once climbing stairs becomes difficult (or unsafe).

Comfort measures include medications that can keep your parents' symptoms under control and allow them to be largely if not completely pain-free. Tremendous advances in pharmaceuticals for pain relief can allow physicians to manage and—in some cases—even remove the pain associated often with disease. Sometimes, however, such medications result in other difficulties. (I still remember my sister complaining about the hidden indignities of cancer—including constipation resulting from codeine and other opioids.) As your parent's illness progresses, you may seek help from a palliative physician who can provide expert guidance on pain and symptom control. Most major cities in North America have palliative services, including pain and symptom management teams. Often such services will visit a patient at home, obviating the need for an office or hospital visit.

As long as your parent is considered "mentally competent," decisions about what treatments and medications they receive remain in their hands. Many people prefer to be as alert and conscious as possible, and therefore request the smallest dosage of pain medication available. This allows them to deal with the pain yet still to interact with their families, make decisions, control their affairs and so on.

For my father, regular blood transfusions became what he termed a "life saver." Though the transfusions could not, of course, save his life, since his bones were no longer capable of producing red blood cells on their own, each transfusion provided him with a "shot in the arm," and a surge of energy (including improved colour, less drowsiness etc.) that might last for a week or more. Eventually he received a unit or two of blood every week or so, depending on the results of each blood test. We will be forever grateful to the haematology unit for their compassionate care, providing him with this treatment which he regarded as "a comfort measure." (His only complaint was that it took so much time out of his day. "Like watching paint dry," he told me, when I came to visit him in the unit one day.)

Controlling symptoms such as nausea and vomiting is essential to the maintenance of independence and dignity. In my sister's case, she endured dreadful nausea (whether caused by the disease or the pain medications we were never sure) and, despite many attempts by her physicians, she vomited nearly every day for the last four months of her life. This meant that she was reluctant to go out of the house (except to the hospital for appointments), lest she need to vomit. Though I had promised her I'd take her to the mall—one of her favourite things in the world was to shop—we were never able to go because of her uncontrollable nausea.

All of the measures discussed here are aspects of palliative care. The goal is not to prolong life (though it sometimes has that effect) but instead to improve the quality of the person's life and to enable them to live with comfort and dignity until their death. Find out what services are available where your parents live. Some of these services may be provided by government agencies, while others are covered by medical insurance or private payers. Ask your parents' doctor about palliative services. Speak to friends who have cared for their own parents. (For additional services, please see the Resource section on the website.)

11

And a time to die

To every thing there is a season,
and a time to every purpose under the heaven:
A time to be born, and a time to die; a time to plant,
and a time to pluck up that which is planted;
A time to kill, and a time to heal;
a time to break down, and a time to build up;
A time to weep, and a time to laugh;
a time to mourn, and a time to dance;
A time to cast away stones, and a time to gather stones together;
a time to embrace, and a time to refrain from embracing;
A time to get, and a time to lose;
a time to keep, and a time to cast away;
A time to rend, and a time to sew;
a time to keep silence, and a time to speak;
A time to love, and a time to hate;
a time of war, and a time of peace.

Ecclesiastes 3 (King James Version)

E ven though you've known that the end was coming, still the finality of death can come as a shock. This really is where you have been heading all along. This is how it ends. And yet, if you and your family have been viewing your parent's illness as a battle to be won at all costs, or hoping that the doctor might have just one more trick up his sleeve, then death can appear to be a failure rather than the natural end to life.

In this chapter, I will talk about how you can prepare yourself and your family for your parent's death. As well, I will talk about how to provide the best care possible for your parent, once a cure or remission is no longer possible. I will explore what options are available for end of life care, and point the way towards conversations you can have with your parents that may ease their transition and comfort them as they prepare to leave behind everything and everyone they know and love.

Preparation for the end

If you've been following the advice in this book, by now you and your parents will have consulted a lawyer and completed the paperwork needed in order to ensure that your parent's wishes regarding end of life care are followed. These include a power of attorney for personal care and property (or designated power of attorney, depending on where you live), and an up-to-date will. (See chapter 9.) If your parent's health has deteriorated quickly, leaving you little time to deal with paperwork, then attend to it now. Ask your parent about what kind of care they might want going forward. If they are certain that they do not want to be resuscitated should they experience cardiac arrest, then ask their doctor for a DNR order: this can be attached to their chart if they are in hospital, or posted in a prominent place in their home. As I indicated earlier, only 5% of elderly people who are resuscitated will survive—and an even smaller percentage of those will recover to their pre-heart attack level of health. In the light of that harsh fact, many elderly people choose to complete a DNR order.

If you have been avoiding these details for fear of upsetting your parents, don't wait any longer! If your parents have no documentation regarding powers of attorney, or if those forms are out-of-date, now is the time to act. For example: your father's sole designation of your mother might have been sensible 25 (or even five) years ago, but now it might need to be updated to include one or more of the adult children.

If your parent has already made arrangements with a funeral home or cemetery, make sure that you know where the documentation is located. While it is never too late to call a funeral home to make arrangements, you will not want to be making such calls while your parent is on their death bed.

Talking about dying with my father

Until his final illness struck, my father had been a powerful person—a corporate lawyer, Justice of the Provincial Supreme Court of Appeal, Head of the Law Society. Even at 92 he had chaired an important legal committee. But now he found himself in unfamiliar, perhaps terrifying, terrain.

"Dad," I said, when I arrived for a visit a month before he died, "You can tell me this is none of my business, but I'm worried about you. You seem depressed and you don't seem to have anything you're looking forward to."

"Well," he said, "I've had visits with a few good friends." (I tried not to resent the fact that he hadn't mentioned my visits or those of my siblings!) "Apart from that, what is there to look forward to?" He paused. "It's not as though anyone comes and sits in that chair you're sitting in and says, 'John, how do you feel about dying? How long do you think you have left?' We all just act as if this were normal."

This was the first time in his illness that he had uttered the word "dying."

"I think we take our lead from you, Dad. Mostly you don't seem to want to talk about dying."

"That's true," he said. "I don't really see that there's anything to say."

"I know you're not the kind of person to talk about your feelings but sometimes people find it helps. If you'd like to, I'd be happy to talk about it."

And so we talked.

"It isn't as though it were a tragedy," he said.

"You mean, your dying?" I asked.

"Yes, it's not as it was with your sister, dying at 51. I'm 94."

"The fact that you're 94 doesn't mean it's not hard," I said.

He looked at me, perplexed.

"Dad, you've had a long time to get used to being in the world. It's not an easy habit to give up."

"I suppose not," he nodded, and turned back to the television.

That was the one and only time we talked about dying.

I suspect you'll have better luck with your parents. Especially if you start early!

I should add that my father had taken care of the funeral arrangements, spoken with his minister regarding music and the homily, and had already purchased a funeral plot for himself and my mother. His financial affairs were in order and his will was in the hands of his lawyer.

Where would you like to die? Options for end of life care

There is no "one size fits all" answer to the needs of dying people and their families. Each death is as unique as the person who is dying, and their needs may change from day to day or moment to moment. As a result, over the course of the dying process, a patient may receive care in a number of different settings.

In North America today, some seven out of ten people indicate that they would like to die at home. And that number has risen steadily in the last two decades. Nonetheless, only three out of ten people actually die at home. Many end up in the emergency room or in an intensive care unit at end of life, arguably the least desirable option and definitely not what most people indicate that they want. Hospitals are designed for acute care needs, where the focus is on treatment and cure, and death itself is a natural process, not an acute care event.

In the United States, one out of every five elderly patients discharged from hospital is readmitted within a month. So common is this experience that researchers and health care administrators are now attempting to address the "revolving door" of ER for elderly people in the final year or months of their lives. I can't remember the number of times my father ended up by himself in the emergency room late in the evening (usually on a holiday weekend) waiting for a transfusion and an examination by the cardiologist on duty. Persuading his haematologist to schedule blood tests and transfusions at regular intervals ended this cycle of exhausting and distressing hospital visits. Changes to the way health care services are delivered to the elderly—from increased home and hospice care to "house calls" from physicians and nurses—are needed to reduce the alarming rate of hospital readmissions and deaths in ERs and ICUs.

What alternatives to acute care hospitals are available for dying people and their families?

The origins of hospice and palliative care

During the late 1960s and 1970s, a movement of people who had first-hand experience of the loss of family members and friends began to question why dying people were being abandoned in hospitals or subjected to extreme (often unnecessary) measures when death was inevitable and close. They found their champions in the pioneers of the hospice palliative care movement.

Perhaps the most significant person to bring death into the public eye in North America was Elisabeth Kübler-Ross, a pioneer in providing psychological counselling to the dying. In her first book, *On Death and Dying* (originally published in 1969), she described five stages she believed were experienced by those nearing death—denial, anger, bargaining, depression, and acceptance. She also suggested that death be considered a normal stage of life, and offered strategies for treating patients and their families as they negotiate these stages. Kübler-Ross's books became bestsellers among physicians and the general public alike, and, though her theory of the stages of dying has been criticized over recent years, her work remains prominent in any discussion about death, dying, and the grieving process.

Credit for championing compassionate care and hospices for dying people goes to Dame Cicely Saunders, a pioneering physician and founder of St. Christopher's House in London, England, in 1967. In her book *Living with Dying: The Management of Terminal Disease,* Dame Cicely explained the philosophy behind her work: "A patient, wherever he may be, should expect the same analytical attention to terminal suffering as he received for the original diagnosis and treatment of his condition. The aim is no longer a cure but the chance of living to his fullest potential in physical ease and activity with the assurance of personal relationships until he dies."

Inspired by visiting and working with Cicely Saunders at St. Christopher's, Dr. Balfour Mount, a urologist and surgical oncologist, piloted a study of the needs of dying patients in Royal Victoria Hospital in Montreal, Canada. Appalled by the suffering he and his team found, Mount established a hospice-like ward within the hospital to relieve suffering and provide quality end of life care. Dr. Mount coined the term "palliative care" *(soins palliatif* in French), an alternative to the word "hospice" which, in French, still carried the stigma as a place of last resort for the poor and derelict. The pilot project also featured "a consultation team to work with other hospital wards, a home-care outreach service, and a bereavement follow-up program." Known as the father of palliative care in North America, Dr. Mount has devoted himself to spreading the message of palliative care throughout his life.

In the United States, hospice services can also be credited to Dame Cicely, whom Florence Wald, Dean of the School of Nursing at Yale University, invited to give a series of lectures in 1963. A decade later, the first hospice service in the United States opened in Branford, Connecticut. Today, as in the pioneering days, hospice focuses on care not cure, with many of the services being provided in the patient's home, particularly in the United States.

In Canada, the terms hospice care and palliative care are used interchangeably to describe services provided by an interdisciplinary team to people with a life-limiting or terminal illness. Such care can be provided within a specialized palliative care unit in a hospital, in a free-standing residential facility, or in a patient's home through visits by community nurses, palliative care physicians, and hospice volunteers. Today, many hospitals have a palliative care unit, and steps are being taken to provide palliative care in the long-term care facilities and nursing homes where large numbers of North Americans spend their final days.

Residential-care hospices

Modeled on Cicely Saunders' work at St. Christopher's House in London, free-standing hospices began to appear in Canada in the 1980s with the establishment of Casey House (a Toronto hospice for AIDS patients, established in 1983). Although relatively few in number, free-standing hospices have become an important model for the delivery of palliative care services, providing an alternative to home care (when medical needs or personal circumstances may make a home death unrealistic) or to acute care in hospital, the most costly, and perhaps least desirable, alternative.

The philosophy of residential hospices mirrors the goals of palliative care—to alleviate pain and suffering, and to allow the dying person to live their final days in comfort and ease amidst the people they love. Both the patient and the family receive support and care from the interdisciplinary hospice team, which includes nurses, personal service workers, physicians (at many hospices, the patients' doctors follow them to the hospice to provide continuing care), social workers, chefs, and administrative and cleaning staff. Residential hospices are also supported by large numbers of volunteers who may assist staff with feeding and repositioning patients, cooking meals, reading to and sitting quietly with patients, as well as assisting with building maintenance, gardening, fundraising events, or working at reception. It is in this setting that I have volunteered for the past 13 years.

The focus of hospice programs is on the entire family, rather than only on the patient. In the residence, family members can visit 24 hours a day, and cots are often provided for them to stay overnight as the end nears. Family members often describe the feeling of a burden being lifted, as they feel able to rely upon the professional care of nurses and personal support workers, and the care of volunteers. Many hospice programs also provide counselling for family members and bereavement support. In Canada, all of these services are provided free of charge.

"Hospices provide a more home-like experience, while costing only about $439 per patient a day, compared to $850 to $1,000 in a hospital bed, and $2908 for an intensive care bed." Although the bed-care cost of a residential care hospice is between a half and a third of the cost of a hospital bed, governments have been relatively slow to get on board to support hospices, perhaps mistakenly fearing that these facilities would add to mushrooming health care costs.

Hospice and palliative care in the US

In the United States, palliative care refers to "patient and family-centered care that optimizes quality of life by anticipating, preventing, and treating suffering." Palliative care services are provided by an interdisciplinary team, and are available from the time a patient receives their diagnosis. Thus, a patient can be undergoing curative or life-prolonging treatment at the same time as they are receiving palliative care services. The cost of these services is not covered by Medicare or Medicaid (but may be under some forms of medical insurance).

In contrast, hospice services are available free of charge to people who have received a prognosis of less than six months to live. While the services are similar in approach and delivery to palliative care, hospice services are paid for by the Medicare or Medicaid hospice benefit. Any person 65 years of age or older with a life expectancy of 6 months or less is eligible for the Medicare benefit. Most people receive these services in their home (including long term care facilities and nursing homes), where they receive pain and symptom management services, drugs, medical supplies and equipment, and emotional, spiritual, and psychosocial care. Although Medicare provides these services for up to six months (and sometimes longer), most people benefit from them for only a short people of time. Perhaps they fear that getting hospice involved means that they are "giving up the ghost," whereas in fact they are accessing services that can enable them to live with greater comfort for their remaining days.

Dying at home

Families and patients seeking an alternative to a hospital-based death have increasingly turned to dying at home as a way to provide comfort, support and familiar surroundings to their loved one. In the United States, most hospice services are delivered in the home by a coordinated team that includes nurses, social workers, volunteers, and allied professionals. With adequate support (including hospice services, nursing support, a palliative care team visiting on a regular basis to attend to medical needs, home health and home support volunteers), the home can provide an excellent alternative to a hospital death. Being at home enables both the family and the patient to have more control over the conditions and circumstances of the patient's care. Playing the music your parent enjoys, whether on a stereo or an instrument, can provide great comfort. Pets, or a favourite grandchild, can climb into bed with your parent, giving them direct touch (or licks!) As well, there is likely to be far more space at home, enabling family and friends to come and go, or to take turns sitting with the patient, rather than crowding into the patient's hospital room. Most importantly, the home can feel safe and familiar, at a potentially frightening and painful time.

Should your parent feel strongly in favour of dying at home, you will need a great deal of discussion, planning and organization. If possible, investigate the services that are available in your parent's community before they are needed. It is advisable that family members convene regular family meetings (in person, via

Skype or telephone conference) in order to coordinate what care their parent will receive.

Caring for a terminally ill person at home can be very taxing, as the physical and emotional demands can be potentially overwhelming. Both the duration of the dying process and its circumstances are unpredictable: medical events (such as uncontrollable pain, vomiting, bowel obstruction, hallucinations, bleeding, seizures etc.) can lead to a family being unable to continue to care at home without emergency medical assistance. Some patients do end up at a residential hospice or acute care hospital when care at home is no longer possible. Families that undertake a home death need to be aware that the demands may outstrip their abilities or resources and are advised to prepare for the fact that they might be unable to satisfy a person's wish to die at home. It is important for families to know that, should they be unable to provide for a home death, it is not their fault. The most important issues are the provision of pain and symptom relief, along with the sense of dignity and care that your parent receives.

Wherever it is delivered—in a palliative care unit in a hospital, in a residential hospice in the community, or in the patient's home—palliative care improves the quality of life of dying people and their families. Furthermore, recent research published in the New England Journal of Medicine has shown that palliative care can actually increase the length of a patient's life.[9]

Key questions

In order to achieve your parents' goals regarding the location of their death and the types of comfort and care that they hope to receive, ongoing conversations (see Chapter 9) about their hopes, wishes, and fears are essential. These questions can help you to guide these discussions:

- What do you hope for?
- What are you afraid of?
- How can I help you?

Signs that the end is near

Perhaps you've asked the doctor how long she thinks your father has left. Most doctors are hesitant to provide a specific prognosis, since the time still remaining depends on many factors. When pressed by anxious family members or the dying person himself, the doctor may say something like, "long weeks or short months." Sometimes the disease is progressing so rapidly, the doctor may indicate that it's only a matter of time, which you can read as somewhere under three months.

Though you're probably not a physician yourself, still there are signs that will indicate that your parent does not have long to live. (These would of course also apply to any dying person.)

Food and drink

Your parent will gradually eat and drink less and less until finally they may refuse all food or drink. This is often an extremely alarming event for family members. A wife who has cooked special meals for her husband in hopes that he will keep on eating, may be devastated when her husband turns away from her special soup. She may try to pressure him to eat, taking his refusal as stubbornness, rather than as a natural outcome of the dying process. The son or daughter who has been patiently bringing supper to their mother throughout her illness may feel lost without that tangible sign of their love and caring being appreciated.

Sometimes family members will attempt to force a patient to drink, believing that without food or drink their loved one will die. The sad fact is that they are going to die. And at a certain point, the body is no longer able to process food or drink. As the body prepares to die, all of the organs begin to shut down, and forcing down food can in fact cause potentially serious and painful adverse effects.

The following article by Jessica Nutik Zitter, M.D. captures beautifully the challenges that family members face in feeding and providing fluids to their loved ones at the end of life.

Choked by Love

Her son was feeding her like she was a little baby. A hospital cafeteria-issued tuna fish sandwich sat atop a soggy swatch of cellophane on the palm of his left hand. In his right was a butter knife that he used to excise tiny chunks of the sandwich. As I entered the room, he proudly gestured to the remaining portion of the sandwich and communicated reassuringly in broken English that he would keep working hard on getting the whole sandwich into his mother. He was part of our team, and his job, he implied, was to contribute to the project of healing his dying mother by nourishing her with love and calories.

She was a 70-year-old Cantonese-speaking woman with aggressive ovarian cancer. She had been receiving hopeful chemotherapy from her oncologist, but it clearly hadn't been working. On her most recent clinic visit, she had become so critically ill that her doctor had abruptly admitted her to the ICU for stabilization, withholding chemotherapy, to the family's consternation.

Until recently, the cancer had lived quietly inside her, preparing its attack slowly and without raising too much alarm. This time, though, it had risen up like a guerrilla army to fight its final, multi-front battle. Fluid around her lungs squeezed like the worst kind of corset so that every breath exhausted her. Cancerous fronds curled around her intestines, distending her abdomen and further compromising her breathing.

And so she lay there, barely able to breathe, intestines obstructed and bursting, every line on her face reading defeat.

Family members frequently feed my patients food, but it is never just food. It is "lumpia, just like he likes it, with roasted pork," or a "mole chicken burrito, not too spicy this time." Beginning with the breast, food is not only physical sustenance, but spiritual and emotional too. It is a pancultural symbol of love, from Chinese and Ethiopian to Jewish and Vietnamese. The dishes have been carefully and lovingly prepared to bring a taste of home into a sterile and frightening place. They are meant as signs of hope, signs of love, signs of reassurance. And not only for the patient, but for the feeder, too.

And yet for all living things, there comes a time when food becomes something different, something unwelcome, even harmful. An obstructed intestine cannot accommodate a tuna fish sandwich. Even chicken broth, the universal healer of all remedies, can increase the pressure in the stomach, causing nausea, vomiting, and stomach pain, as well as impeding breathing.

That this elderly Chinese woman was being fed a tuna fish sandwich by her son attested to the desperation he must have felt at that moment. Hospital tuna fish sandwiches are rarely eaten by little women from the Chinese mainland. He was caught off-guard by her abrupt transfer from the outpatient oncology clinic into the intensive care unit. He hadn't had time to prepare a special dish.

Her face showed sheer exhaustion as her worried son pushed bite after bite of the foreign substance into her mouth. As with so many patients with advanced illness, food, once enjoyed, was now a burden. Her body had lost the ability to process it, and hunger was a thing of the past.

Yet her son was desperate to love her, and this was all he knew how to do.

Worried, I gently coaxed the sandwich away from him. He nodded vigorously as I tried to explain the risk of feeding. But I couldn't climb our Tower of Babel. I made the universal "I'll be right back" sign and ran off to find an interpreter.

But before I had found one, I heard the familiar crackling words over the PA: "Code Blue, 5th Floor." She had indeed aspirated the sandwich. Her already strangled lungs had been filled with what is often a toxin for a dying body—food.

In feeding our dying loved ones, we are feeding ourselves, warding off our own fear of loss. But when physical life begins to pass, we must learn to transfer our love and support into a different medium. The tuna fish sandwich was a desperate act from a desperate son who wanted to love and honor his mother. But his effort in fact may have shortened her life and caused unintended distress and suffering. When food stops being love and starts being dangerous, it doesn't matter whether it's a bowl of grits, matzo ball soup, or a cafeteria tuna fish sandwich, it is time for us to pull back and discover new ways to sustain ourselves and our loved one.

When your parent is no longer able to take food or drink, ask the doctor or hospice nurse if they can tolerate ice chips or a Popsicle. If they are not able to swallow, a swab dabbed lightly with club soda or a special hydrating spray can be used in order to keep their mouth moistened.

Visions, voices, and visitors

It is not uncommon as someone nears the end of their life for them to speak about having had a visit from someone who has already died. They might describe a visit from their mother or father, a sibling or a child who has gone before them, reassuring them about the process of dying and beyond. Family members may be confused by such stories, wondering if they are a sign of delirium or merely a result of the medications the patient is receiving.

Given that such visits are generally reassuring rather than frightening for the patient, most experts urge family members to listen, rather than to question, or to seek to correct. Just let them talk about their visit with their mother or son, accepting that this is their experience, and enjoy it with them. For some patients, these visits (and voices) can continue for some time and the patient will report that their family member is waiting for them on the other side. The fact is that none of us really knows what happens after death. How reassuring it must be for a dying person to know that they will have familiar faces to welcome them!

One of the first patients I spent time with at the hospice began to report seeing unfamiliar phenomena and feeling strange sensations. "The air is changing. Can you feel it?" she asked me. I was taken aback, as this was my first experience with such things. "Um, no," I said, being scrupulously honest. "Well, I read about it in the *Toronto Star*," she said, "and I can feel it in the air." She began to tell me about the elaborate workings of a strange machine she was building. Although I could not see the machine, this time I had the good sense to ask her to describe it to me, which she did with great enthusiasm.

Later that day, I found myself chatting about these experiences with members of her family. "Did she tell you about the machine she's building? She has never had one bit of mechanical interest or ability in her entire life. And what she's describing she has no business knowing about!" her son told me.

We agreed that these stories were certainly mysterious, and that there was no merit in denying her experiences. Perhaps they were the result of changes in her blood oxygen levels or of her medication. I prefer to see them as another aspect of the mystery of death.

On occasion, dying people will have violent hallucinations, causing them great distress. The patient might yell and flail about, seemingly attempting to beat off an intruder. Here, the physician typically prescribes anti-anxiety medication or a sedative to ease the patient's experience. As hallucinations can be induced by medication, the physician may also adjust the amount or type of medication the patient is receiving.

"Call me a taxi!"

One of the most mystifying occurrences at end of life is the relatively common request by the patient to help them to prepare for their journey. Sometimes this can be very direct. A friend told me that her partner insisted that she get her a bus ticket, put on her slippers, and help her pack her bag shortly before she died. Hospice patients have directed me to call them a cab, book a flight, and ensure that the boat doesn't leave without them. A number have insisted that I locate their slippers and help them get up out of bed—not a good plan for someone who has been bedridden for weeks! Though it can be an unnerving experience for family, and regardless of what it might mean, it represents that the person is preparing to die. Responding in a calm manner, with reassurances that their loved one will be there soon or that you're going to stay with them now, can prevent such requests from turning into potentially dangerous situations.

Sleep

As a person prepares to die, he or she will spend longer and longer stretches of time sleeping. Often patients will withdraw into themselves as their world becomes smaller and smaller. This is not an indication of giving up or anger or avoidance or depression. Dying is hard work! Allow them to sleep, and when they are awake, take advantage of the precious time you have. Sometimes family members attempt to rouse a patient who is somnolent, in hopes of being able to engage in discussion. Occasionally they will ask a physician to reduce the patient's pain medication, believing that it's the medication that is causing them to sleep so much. If you find yourself thinking this way, you might ask yourself whether your need to speak with your parent trumps the importance of their pain being properly contained.

Conversations

For the most part, dying people know that they are dying, whether you or their doctor or anyone else has told them. Don't pretend that they are not dying or avoid their questions or comments about the end. At the hospice, patients will often talk to me about what comes next, occasionally asking me what I think will happen. Here I rely on my own experience with hundreds of hospice patients in telling them that in all likelihood they will simply sleep more and more until finally they die in peace.

Most people are not afraid of death: they are afraid of dying. Regardless of what they think might happen after they are gone, it is the prospect of dying in great pain, or feeling as though they are suffocating, that is of much greater concern to them.

If people ask me what I think happens after death, I respond by asking them what they think happens. Often people have a feeling about what happens and they are simply looking to put that feeling into words. If they push me to speculate, I say that for me, death truly is a mystery.

One of the most important aspects of these last conversations is to give your parent the opportunity to say what they think or feel. This is not the time to dispute their views. Even if your parent says that they think they'll be punished in hell, perhaps you can ask them to talk further about that fear. And you can certainly reassure them that they've been a wonderful parent—assuming that this was at least partly true for you!

Sometimes people will express regrets as they approach death. Let them express these feelings, even if they seem patently unfounded to you. The one regret my sister expressed was that she shouldn't have been so mean. When I challenged her on this (since I found her to be an incredibly kind person, as well as a devoted sister and teacher), she said simply, "Yes, I was." And we left it at that. I'll admit that that observation has remained with me all these years later, and when I find myself being mean to someone or saying something catty, I can hear Carol saying, "Don't be so mean!"

Saying farewell

If your parent remains awake and conscious for some portion of the day, you might ask them if there is anyone they would like to see. While most people seem to prefer the company of their immediate family in their final days, a significant number welcome visitors into their room for as long as they are able to indicate their preference. Perhaps they'd like to see their minister, priest, rabbi, or some other spiritual adviser. Ask them, and then ensure that the visit takes place as soon as possible.

Your parents may have items they wish to pass on to their

children or grandchildren. Be prepared with a pad and paper so that you can record their instructions. Perhaps they want you to convey a message to someone that they haven't been able to see. These acts can help your parent achieve a form of closure before dying.

Memorials and funerals

Your parents may have already made arrangements for their funeral. In this case, you need to know where those instructions are, so that you can act upon them. My father had arranged for his minister to conduct the service, and they had spoken at length about its content. The choir master had been asked to sing the 23rd Psalm and my father had specified a number of hymns that he wished the choir and congregation to sing. When I asked him if he would like any of his daughters to speak, he told me, in his characteristically cryptic style, "You did a very good job at Carol's memorial." (That was his roundabout way of asking me if I would do the same for him!) It was a great relief for us that my father had been so clear about his wishes before he died.

Whatever your parent might request, remember that a memorial or funeral is as much for the living as for the recently dead themselves. Whether it is a religious service or a celebration of life, it allows family and friends a chance to gather and remember the person they loved, and can be an important step in bringing a sense of closure to their death. It is also a time to honour your parents, to celebrate the life they lived, and to reflect upon their influence in your life. It's a time to tell stories, to hold one another, to cry, and to console.

Should I be there when my parent dies?

"My father's in a coma," a friend tells me. "He won't even know if I'm there or not. Should I go?"

This is one of the most common questions that adult children ask when their parent is dying. For people who live far from their parents, and who have probably travelled back and forth from home many times already, it can be a difficult decision to make.

Medical experts confirm that hearing is the last sense to go when a person is dying. While your parent may seem unaware of your presence, it is likely that he can hear your voice, and perhaps be reassured by your presence. Talk to your parent, read to them, tell them you love them. If you can carry a tune (or even if you can't), sing to them.

Does that mean that you have to be by their side? Not necessarily. It depends on what the dying person wants. In my case, my sister repeatedly told me that she wanted me to be there when she died. Even though I was afraid of what it might be like, I promised that I would be there. And I was.

When I asked my father whether he wanted any of his daughters with him when he died, he said no. He just wanted to know that he wouldn't die alone.

If you are comfortable with this, ask your parent whom they want with them at the end. While you can't promise that all of those people can be in attendance, you can certainly let them know your parent's wishes.

I just left the room for a minute. Why didn't she wait for me?

Sons and daughters, husbands and wives sometimes express enormous regret if they're not present for the moment of death. Sometimes it's as simple as going to the washroom and, in that minute, the person takes their last breath.

"I think she was trying to protect you," I reassured my niece, who had been sitting with my Mom for hours. (She felt terrible that she hadn't been with her Granny at the moment when she died.)

I have witnessed this phenomenon so many times at the hospice that I am convinced that people can sometimes control the time of their death. For example, I have seen countless people wait for a son or daughter or grandchild to fly into town before they breathe their final breaths. I suspect that you have heard those stories as well.

No matter what happens, I urge you to think about what matters most to you. How do you want to show up in these last weeks and days of your parent's life? What do you want to say? If you live nearby, perhaps you do want to be with your parent when they die. But there is no rule. The most important thing is to spend time with your parent *before* they die, talking and sharing as best you can, and telling them the things you need to say.

What is he holding on for?

Sometimes a person will continue to linger long after the estimated time frame the doctor has provided. At the hospice, I have seen parents continue to live, despite having taken no food or drink for weeks. For family members, this can be exhausting, as they spend day and night by their loved one's bed, waiting until they die. Although you can never know for what reason why your parent is holding on, you can ease their transition by reassuring them that you will be all right, and that you and your siblings will all help to take care of the parent who will be left behind. Grant them permission to go. Tell them that you will miss them enormously and that you and your family will be OK. And then let them go.

The final breath

Like most Baby Boomers, I spent almost 50 years of my life without seeing a dead body or being with someone as they died. This would have been unheard of 100 years ago and earlier, when death still took place at home, and young children were accustomed to seeing the body of a deceased relative laid to rest in the parlour, for friends and neighbors to view. My own inexperience, which resulted from a deep fear and aversion to death, seems laughable to me now, as I voluntarily spend four hours a week in the company of people who are dying. I helped hospice staff wash both my father- and mother-in-law after they died at home, not to mention countless others at the residential hospice where I volunteer. Death is no longer scary to me, and once again I have my sister to thank.

Though I had reassured my sister many times that her end would most likely be peaceful, I still harboured fears that it might not. What if I was wrong? More importantly (for me), what if I couldn't handle it and went screaming out of the room? Though I never shared that fear with Carol (or anyone else!) I held it right until that final day.

Though I can't predict how your parents' deaths will be (and it will depend upon disease, condition, and location of death among other factors) I can offer some guidance as to the typical pattern. As I've suggested, your parent will begin to sleep more and more, and take in less and less food and drink until finally only mouth care is provided. Despite movie depictions of deep and meaningful death bed conversations, it is far more likely that your parent will fall into a deep sleep from which they are unlikely to wake up. Prior to death, your parent may experience a period of Cheyne-Stokes respiration (sometimes referred to as the death rattle), characterized by a deep, noisy breathing followed by increasing periods of apnea (absence of breathing). The noise of the "death rattle" can be disturbing when you first hear it. In the case of my sister, her breathing had changed after I had left the previous night and seemed to fill the room when I arrived early the next morning. When I asked the palliative nurse, she explained what was happening and reassured me that it was not uncomfortable for my sister. Sometimes doctors will give the patient some medication to dry up the secretions, she told me, but it's mainly for the family's benefit because they find the noise so disturbing. She won't even be aware that it's happening. Hearing that, I was able to settle down and be with my sister. Her breathing eased almost immediately.

Since that time, I have sat with a number of patients whose breathing echoed down the hall. Each time, I could reassure the family that it was not painful for their loved one, and that it was a signal that the end was close.

It is a humbling experience, being with someone as they take their last breaths. Gradually the gap between breaths increases, until a full minute or two has passed without an inhalation. I can still remember thinking, "that's it" after more than one long stretch of silence from Carol. And then she would gasp again, inhaling the breath into her lungs. Until finally it was the last breath, and I sat for a few minutes in utter silence, taking in the finality of her death. "Thanks for making it not scary," I said to her after she was gone. It was her final gift to me, one I can share with others, in my hospice work and in my writing.

12

Aftermath: death and
the meaning of life

Life and death are of supreme importance.
Time passes swiftly and opportunity is lost.
Let us awaken, awaken,
Do not squander your life.
—Zen Evening Chant

After it's all done, after your parent has taken their last breath, after the paperwork, funeral and wake, the thank you letters, the reassuring platitudes ("He had a good long life," "At least his suffering is over," "She's in a better place") you may well wonder: What just happened? What do we do now? What will my life be like without my parents? What does "family" look like without them?

Suddenly you are the oldest generation—without your buffer against mortality. Your safety net is gone, your repository of memories, the person who loved you completely. This was possibly the only person who knew you for your entire life and now she is gone.

Or perhaps he was a tyrant, always finding ways to belittle you, or worse yet, to abuse you. Perhaps she was always finding fault with you, even when you were caring for her in her final years.

No matter what your relationship with your parents was like, once they are dead that relationship is over. There are no more second chances to get it right. No more opportunities to say what you need to say, to hear their stories, to ask questions about family photos and history.

The finality of death will grab you not just once but over and over again, often when you least expect it. You might be walking down the street and catch a glimpse of someone who wears a hat just like your Dad did. You might be thinking about making meatloaf for supper and find yourself crying as you remember all those suppers your Mom cooked for the family. If you called her every Sunday, you might find yourself picking up the phone and starting to dial her number. At night, you might dream that you've been having dinner together, and wake up crying when you realize that she is gone.

You are probably exhausted, especially if your parent's final journey was a lengthy one. You long for a nap in the afternoon, but you are so far behind in so many areas of your life that you feel as though you have no time to rest. You worry that it's time to pick up the pieces of the life you more or less left behind when caregiving took over.

Before you go racing off in a million directions all at once, I urge you to take some time to grieve your loss and to consider the things you've learned along the way.

Grief, like dying itself, is hard work. You will need help—ask for it and accept it. People will bring meals by the house, offer to run errands for you, arrange play dates with your children. Let people help you. Friends who have lost their own parents will know how hard this stage of life is. Those who haven't probably suspect that their time is not far off. Perhaps, as a community, we can grieve.

Tell others your story. People who care about you will be more than willing to listen, especially in the first few weeks after your parent's death. You may find that some people back away when you answer "still having a rough time" when they casually ask how you're doing. Let them go. Like them, I used to be afraid that someone who had experienced death was somehow contagious.

Open yourself up to others in your situation—people who have lost someone close to them or who are caring for an elderly parent or loved one. Share what you've learned. Those lessons, delivered in a humane, compassionate manner, will be of enormous help to others.

What will become of your family?

Without your parents, are you and your siblings still a family? Will you continue the holiday traditions now that your parents are gone? You've rallied when your parents were ill and dying, phoned and emailed each other, arranged schedules, pulled together. But now, without them, what family arrangements, if any, do you want to continue? There is no right answer to these questions. For some families, the connections forged during their parents' final years will have drawn them closer together and they will continue to mark birthdays, seasonal events, the addition of grandchildren, and other important events. For others, siblings may drift apart once the bond that held them together is severed.

How do you want to honour your parents?

There are countless ways in which you can honour your parents. If you were able to talk to them about their wishes before their death, then you may already know what they wanted. Establishing an award or prize in their name, planting a tree or placing a bench in their honour, asking friends and family to donate to their favourite charity, are all ways to honour their contributions and keep alive their memory. You and your siblings might wish to write a Lives Lived column for the local paper. On a more personal level, you might wish to establish a ritual in your own life (e.g. having a special meal on their birthday, connecting with your siblings on the date of their death, or running a marathon in their memory). Although it used to be frowned upon as morbid, many people now keep a photograph of their parent on their desk. For me, writing about my father has helped me to keep his memory vivid and alive.

Whatever method you choose, perhaps the most important way to honour them is in how you live your life.

What have you learned? How will you live your life differently?

Did your father's independence and refusal to "go gentle into that good night" inspire you to emulate his strength and ferocity? Or did it make you want to open up to vulnerability and interdependence? What about your mother's grace and dignity in the face of a life she might never have chosen?

Throughout this book I have posed a central question: How do you want to show up for your parents during the final phase of their lives? The corollary to that question is: How do you want to show up for the rest of *your* life?

Answering those questions will, of necessity, require self-examination and exploration, even soul-searching.

Talk with your spouse, your children, your siblings, about what you have learned. Tell them what matters most to you. Explore how they might help you. Get your affairs in order now.

Begin to incorporate the lessons that you've learned in caring for your parents into your life. All too easily you can get caught up in work and domestic demands and forget the importance of being present, slowing down, simply being.

Losing your parents provides you with an opportunity to consider making important changes in your life. Perhaps you have thought about moving to another city, but put it off so you could be close by when your parents needed you. Perhaps you turned down a promotion at work because caregiving was taking up so much of your time. There may be classes or lessons you'd always thought about taking, if only you had the time. Now you do.

What were the things your parents wished they had done, if only they'd had the chance? Did they have regrets? What might your regrets be if you were to die tomorrow? How can you turn those regrets into positive changes in your life? (Hint: people who are dying rarely express the wish that they'd worked more hours or spent less time with their children.)

Right now it may be hard to imagine your life after loss. That's where coaching comes in. Working together, we can uncover the dreams you may have abandoned many years ago. We can begin to make sense of what you've learned—see the ways you've grown—not denying your loss but building upon it. In my own life, it was my calling to do hospice work. "You're going to be an expert at this by the time you're done with me," my sister asserted. The lessons she taught led me to become a hospice volunteer four years after her death, work that I am still doing thirteen years later.

A few months after my mother died, I submitted an article to the Canadian Broadcasting Corporation which was hosting a series of "This I Believe" programmes. I had been writing all that winter, churning out hundreds of pages, and it seemed like a great challenge to write about my sister in one page or less.

I was thrilled when my piece was accepted and a few days later I headed downtown to the radio studio to tape my story. When I left the studio and walked out into the bright summer's day, suddenly I found tears rolling down my cheeks. "Carol and Mom and Dad would be so proud of me!" I said aloud. I walked the long block to my car, crying, feeling their loss deeply.

You will probably experience moments like this throughout your remaining years, long after your parents have died. Despite received wisdom, we never really get over the significant losses in our lives. Rather, we are transformed by them in ways we can't possibly imagine. That is, if we let ourselves feel the deep sadness and open up to the resulting changes.

If I have conveyed one thing in this book, I hope it is the message that you *do* have time for this. Time for your parents, time for your children, time to show up for the things that really matter in your life. Time for death—but time for life too.

Acknowledgments

The genesis of this book lies in my experiences of providing care for my sister Carol and my parents, John and Dora Arnup, when they were dying. Writing became a way for me to come to terms with their deaths and to make sense of the lessons I was learning. I began to write about my sister in 2001, not coincidentally, the same year that I took the volunteer training course at a local hospice.

Over the years, many people have encouraged and supported my writing. My daughters, Jesse and Katie (as long as I wasn't writing about them!), my partner Nancy (even though I was writing about her!), my coach David Hoe (who helped me to trust my inner wisdom), Alice McVeigh (editor extraordinaire), Janet Tingwald (for kicking my butt when I needed it), Don Carroll (who understands the writing life), and Sheridan and Stan of Meadowlark (for the care and skill they brought to my words). Koshin and Chodo, co-founders of the New York Zen Center for Contemplative Care, provided inspiration, wisdom, and powerful teachings.

I would like to offer my enormous gratitude to the people who entrusted me with their stories. And to the patients and families I have had the privilege of serving at the hospice—your courage and compassion continue to inspire me every week.

Writing Fellowships from the Virginia Center for the

Creative Arts provided me with the gift of uninterrupted time, solitude, and support I needed to dig deeply into my experiences with death and dying. In addition, I received writing residencies at the Banff Centre for the Arts and the Vermont Studio Center. I am grateful to Deborah Dionne, manager of the Cape Codder Guest House, who has maintained a safe haven for me in Room 2 every year.

As readers of this book will know, I like to write in bars. Thanks to the staff at Fanizzi's (Provincetown), Patty's (Ottawa), and the Briar Patch (Amherst VA)—especially to Jim, who always greets me, whenever I return: "How's the writing going, Katherine? Still writing about death and dying?"

Special thanks to Nancy Wasserman, my biggest fan, first reader, and companion in joy and sorrow.

Notes

P. 13: "The average Canadian born in 2009 ..." Conference
Board of Canada, *How Canada Performs* (2009). http://www.
conferenceboard.ca/hcp/details/health/life-expectancy.aspx

P. 14: "As a recent Princeton University study confirmed ..."
Angelina Grigoryeva, Department of Sociology, Office of
Population Research, Princeton University, "When Gender
Trumps Everything: The Division of Parent Care Among
Siblings." Presented at the American Sociological Associa-
tion, August 2014. I am grateful to the author for providing
me with a copy of her paper.

P. 22: "According to the National Highway Traffic ..." Cited in
Jim Henry, "Tough Assignment: Talking to Elderly Parents
about Their Driving," *Forbes Magazine*, June 13, 2014. http://
www.forbes.com/sites/jimhenry/2014/06/30/tough-assignment-
talking-to-elderly-parents-about-their-driving/

P. 22: "A fascinating survey of 1000 people ..." Henry, "Tough
Assignment: Talking to Elderly Parents about Their Driving."

P. 50: "Increasingly, neurological research demonstrates ..."
Susan Weinschenk, PhD, "The True Cost Of Multi-Tasking:
You could be losing up to 40% of your productivity," *Psychol-
ogy Today*, September 18, 2012. http://www.psychologytoday.
com/blog/brain-wise/201209/the-true-cost-multi-tasking

P. 87: "Health care and elder care systems …" Angelina Grigoryeva, "When Gender Trumps Everything: The Division of Parent Care Among Siblings." Presented at the American Sociological Association, August 2014.

P. 90: "Nonetheless, health care remains …" Jonnelle Marte, "Health care is often the biggest expense in retirement—and the hardest to predict," *Washington Post* (online), September 15, 2014, using data from the study by caring.com, released September 2014. https://www.caring.com/research/senior-care-cost-index-2014

P. 90: "A survey conducted for …" PNC Financial Services Group, *Perspectives on Retirement Survey* (Fall 2014). https://www.pnc.com/content/dam/pnc-com/pdf/aboutpnc/PressKits/RetirementSurveys/2014_0918_Retirement%20Survey_Summary.pdf

P. 93: "In recent years, young people …" See Grant Charles, Tim Stainton, and Sheila Marshall, *Young Carers in Canada: The Hidden Costs and Benefits of Caregiving,* http://www.vanierinstitute.ca/modules/news/newsitem.php?ItemId=444#. UgJbcW2f2aY

P. 95: "For a brilliant, humorous …" Roz Chast, *Can't We Talk about Something More Pleasant?* New York: Bloomsbury, 2014.

P. 95: "It is estimated that …" Shanta R. Dube, MPH, Robert F. Anda, MD, MS, Charles L. Whitfield, MD, David W. Brown, MSPH, MS, Vincent J. Felitti, MD, Maxia Dong, MD, PhD, Wayne H. Giles, MD, MS, "Long-Term Consequences of Childhood Sexual Abuse by Gender of Victim." *American Journal of Preventative Medicine* 2005;28(5):430–38

P. 96: "Currently, there are approximately …" Alzheimer's Association, 2014 *Alzheimer's Disease Facts and Figures.* http://www.alz.org/downloads/Facts_Figures_2014.pdf

P. 96: "The financial toll of Alzheimer's ..." Alzheimer's Association, 2014 *Alzheimer's Disease Facts and Figures.*

P. 104: "It's always too soon ..." The Conversation Project, http:// theconversationproject.org/its-always-too-soon-until-its-too-late-advanced-care-planning-with-alzheimers/

P. 107: "Despite what you might think ..." See article in *USA Today*, citing surveys conducted by Liberty Mutual. http:// www.usatoday.com/story/news/nation/2014/06/24/senior-drivers-willing-to-talk/11281195/

P. 112: "Misconceptions about Advance ..." Used by permission of the American Bar Association, December 2014. See "Myths and Facts about Advance Health Care Directives." http://www.americanbar.org/content/dam/aba/migrated/Commissions/myths_fact_hc_ad.authcheckdam.pdf. The version that appears here is taken from an adaptation by the Family Caregiver Alliance (November 2014). http://www.helpguide. org/articles/aging-well/advanced-health-care-directives-and-living-wills.htm

P. 113: "The Family Caregiver Alliance ..." Family Caregiver Alliance (November 2014): http://www.helpguide.org/articles/ aging-well/advanced-health-care-directives-and-living-wills. htm. Used by permission.

P. 113: "When I asked my students ..." Katherine Arnup, "Lessons in Death and Dying," *Journal of Palliative Care* 25 (2) 2009, 109–10.

P. 157: "Where would you like to die? ..." Portions of this section appeared in Katherine Arnup, *Death, Dying, and Canadian Families* (Ottawa: Vanier Institute of the Family), November 2013. http://www.vanierinstitute.ca/include/get.php?nodeid=33 30&format=download

P. 157: "So common is this experience …" Robert Wood Johnson Foundation, *The Revolving Door: A Report on US Hospital Readmissions,* February 2013. http://www.rwjf.org/content/dam/farm/reports/reports/2013/rwjf404178

P. 158: "In her book *Living with Dying* …" Dame Cicely Saunders, "Living with Dying: The Management of Terminal Disease," cited in Heather Robertson, *Meeting Death: In Hospital, Hospice, and at Home,* Toronto: McClelland and Stewart, 2000, 69.

P. 159: "Dr. Mount coined the term …" The word "palliative" is derived from the Latin word *palliare* meaning "to cover or cloak."

P. 159: "The pilot project also featured …" "A Moral Force: The Story of Dr. Balfour Mount," *The Ottawa Citizen,* April 25, 2005.

P. 159: "In the United States, hospice services …" Dennis Hevesi, "Florence S. Wald, American Pioneer in End-of-Life Care, Is Dead at 91." *New York Times,* November 14, 2008. http://www.nytimes.com/2008/11/14/health/14wald.html?_r=1&

P. 161: "Hospices provide a more …" Lisa Priest, "To Go Gently into That Good Night: When Quality of Death Can Enhance Quality of Life," *The Globe and Mail,* March 1, 2012.

P. 161: "In the United States, palliative care…" National Consensus Project for Quality Palliative Care, *Clinical Practice Guidelines for Quality Palliative Care, Second Edition,* 2009. http://www.nationalconsensusproject.org/guideline.pdf

P. 163: "Wherever it is delivered …" Jennifer S. Temel, M.D., Joseph A. Greer, Ph.D., Alona Muzikansky, M.A., Emily R. Gallagher, R.N., Sonal Admane, M.B., B.S., M.P.H., Vicki A. Jackson, M.D., M.P.H., Constance M. Dahlin, A.P.N.,

Craig D. Blinderman, M.D., Juliet Jacobsen, M.D., William F. Pirl, M.D., M.P.H., J. Andrew Billings, M.D., and Thomas J. Lynch, M.D., "Early Palliative Care for Patients with Metastatic Non–Small-Cell Lung Cancer," *New England Journal of Medicine* 363 (2010):733-742.

P. 165: "Choked by Love ..." Jessica Nutik Zitter, M.D. "Choked by Love," posted on her blog *At the Intersection of Quantity and Quality*, October 18, 2014. I am grateful to Jessica for granting me permission to reprint this post in its entirety. http://jessicazitter.com/choked-love/ For another excellent article on the dangers of feeding patients at the end of life, see Jessica Nutik Zitter, M.D., "Food and the Dying Patient," *New York Times Wellness Blog*, August 21, 2014. http://well.blogs.nytimes.com/2014/08/21/food-and-the-dying-patient/?_php=true&_type=blogs&_r=0

About the Author

Katherine Arnup, PhD is a cultural analyst, social historian, life coach, and retired university professor. She is the author of the award-winning book, *Education for Motherhood: Advice for Mothers in Twentieth-Century Canada*, editor of the first book on lesbian families in Canada *(Lesbian Parenting: Living with Pride and Prejudice)*, and author of more than three dozen articles on marriage, motherhood, lesbian and gay families, aging, and death and dying. Her research study, *Death, Dying, and Canadian Families*, was published by the Vanier Institute of the Family in 2013. She writes a blog on hospice volunteering. www.hospicevolunteering. wordpress.com

Katherine's coaching practice, Life Changes Coaching, provides compassionate, caring, and courageous support for people dealing with major transitions and for families and individuals dealing with aging, illness, and end of life issues. She is deeply committed to bringing discussions about death and dying into the public sphere. She has been a keynote speaker at international conferences and is a frequent media commentator on end of life issues.

She lives in Ottawa, Canada.

Contact Katherine at katherine@katherinearnup.com

To view the resource section of this book,

see www.katherinearnup.com